# The Spirit of Everything

*Awakening to a Miraculous Life*

SHARON JOGERST

BALBOA
PRESS
A DIVISION OF HAY HOUSE

Copyright © 2019 Sharon Jogerst.

All rights reserved. No part of this book may be used or reproduced by any means, graphic, electronic, or mechanical, including photocopying, recording, taping or by any information storage retrieval system without the written permission of the author except in the case of brief quotations embodied in critical articles and reviews.

Author Credits: contributing author of "Soulmates with Paws, Hooves and Wings"

Cover Art , Interior Photos and Graphics/Art Credit: Sharon Jogerst

Balboa Press books may be ordered through booksellers or by contacting:

Balboa Press
A Division of Hay House
1663 Liberty Drive
Bloomington, IN 47403
www.balboapress.com
1 (877) 407-4847

"This is a work of creative nonfiction. While all the stories in this book are true, some names and identifying details have been changed to protect the privacy of the people involved."

Because of the dynamic nature of the Internet, any web addresses or links contained in this book may have changed since publication and may no longer be valid. The views expressed in this work are solely those of the author and do not necessarily reflect the views of the publisher, and the publisher hereby disclaims any responsibility for them.

The author of this book does not dispense medical advice or prescribe the use of any technique as a form of treatment for physical, emotional, or medical problems without the advice of a physician, either directly or indirectly. The intent of the author is only to offer information of a general nature to help you in your quest for emotional and spiritual well-being. In the event you use any of the information in this book for yourself, which is your constitutional right, the author and the publisher assume no responsibility for your actions.

Print information available on the last page.

ISBN: 978-1-9822-2608-4 (sc)
ISBN: 978-1-9822-2610-7 (hc)
ISBN: 978-1-9822-2609-1 (e)

Library of Congress Control Number: 2019904354

Balboa Press rev. date: 05/09/2019

*This book is dedicated to the unlimited
beings of light that we are,
floating together on the cosmic sea...*

*"Listen, O drop; give yourself up without regret,
and in exchange gain the Ocean.
Listen O drop; bestow upon yourself this honor,
and in the arms of the Sea be secure."*
-Rumi

# Contents

Evocation ................................................................................. xi
Introduction ........................................................................... xiii

## Part One
### Shattering the Great Illusion

| | | |
|---|---|---|
| Chapter 1 | Floating Beyond Form | 1 |
| Chapter 2 | A Child's Intuition | 5 |
| Chapter 3 | The Mystery of Dreams | 11 |
| Chapter 4 | Lessons in Creating Reality | 19 |
| Chapter 5 | Angelic Intervention | 25 |
| Chapter 6 | Between Worlds | 33 |
| Chapter 7 | Corridors of Time | 39 |
| Chapter 8 | Animal Soul Friends | 45 |
| Chapter 9 | Whisperings from the Universe | 59 |

## Part Two
### Spiritual Alchemy

| | | |
|---|---|---|
| Chapter 10 | Dissolving the Dream of What is Not True | 67 |
| Chapter 11 | Winds of Karma | 77 |
| Chapter 12 | Your Energetic Signature | 83 |
| Chapter 13 | Understanding Brain Wave Frequencies | 89 |
| Chapter 14 | How to Use Your Mind to Alter Reality | 97 |
| Chapter 15 | Rising Above the World of Duality | 103 |
| Chapter 16 | Connect with Your Angels and Spirit Guides | 109 |
| Chapter 17 | The Conscious Intelligence of the Body | 115 |
| Chapter 18 | Self-Love and the Freedom of Forgiveness | 121 |

| | | |
|---|---|---|
| Chapter 19 | Energetic Healing for Yourself and Others | 129 |
| Chapter 20 | Understanding Chakras, Auras, and the Light Body | 135 |
| Chapter 21 | How to See and Read Auras | 147 |
| Chapter 22 | Creating Your Future | 153 |
| Chapter 23 | Healing Your Past | 157 |
| Chapter 24 | Infinite Abundance | 163 |
| Chapter 25 | Lead With Your Heart | 169 |
| Chapter 26 | Raise Your Vibration | 175 |

A Note to the Reader ............ 183

# Evocation

In the luminous realm of souls, on the shores of the great, shining crystalline sea; a gentle Being stands at the water's edge, gathering up the sparkles of reflected sunlight as the waves rush in. Each dazzling droplet is a spark of God; a soul waiting to make the journey to the worlds below.

Stooping down tenderly, the ethereal Being picks up some sand made of crushed iridescent pearls, and carefully molds a small vessel. Then, selecting a tiny droplet of twinkling light, the Being places the radiant spark inside the glimmering vessel and whispers, "My beloved Sparkle, take your light with you. Use it to heal the broken hearts of the suffering and hopeless souls who have lost their way and forgotten the truth of who they really are. Your light is your tether to the infinite realms, ensuring that you will always be connected to your celestial home. Strive to remain conscious as you enter the worlds of density and matter; for if you ever forget your light, you will easily falter and fall into the illusion of powerlessness. Everything that you desire will be accessible to you, as long as you remember your origin and the Great Ocean of Love and Mercy, from whence you came."

With a loving kiss, the benevolent Being turned toward the glistening, ethereal river that flows from the crystalline sea, and gently set the vessel down with Sparkle inside. The river was an infinite stream of shimmering lights, made up of souls on their way to begin a new life. Together they bobbled and sailed, pulled along by the current that flowed outward and onward towards planet Earth.

As the journey continued; gradually the shining river became a river of stars, and Sparkle was catapulted through space. Going faster and faster and gathering density, a body began to form around the vessel of light. Then, there was a gentle floating feeling, until at last, everything grew dark and silent. Only Sparkle's radiance remained to illuminate the night.

Sparkle waited indefinitely in solitude, unaware of what was to happen next. Finally, there was a sudden rousing movement, and Sparkle felt herself being pushed and propelled forcefully through a dark canal. Then, with one final thrust, she arrived abruptly; gasping for air on planet Earth, wrapped in the pure innocence of a newborn baby.

Sparkle laid in the darkness with her eyes tightly closed, feeling utterly confused, disoriented, and abandoned. Then, suddenly, a tiny point of light appeared from within Sparkle's mind. She watched with excitement as glittering, brilliant rays spread into an ever-widening circle that seemed to fill the whole Universe. In her inner vision, Sparkle saw the luminous Being once more; standing in the center of the encircling glow, gazing at her with compassionate eyes and outstretched hands. All at once, a stream of light flowed out like a river from within the tiny infant's beating heart, and merged with the all-encompassing Universal Light.

The benevolent Being embraced Sparkle and spoke to her tenderly with reassurance, "My beloved child, you are not alone. I am always with you, as close as your breath. You have a mission to fulfill on Earth. Take your light with you to shine in the darkness. Always remember who you truly are. Illuminate the way for others; for now, you are a walking star."

# Introduction

Greetings! Namaste! Soul Traveler! The Spirit in me greets the Spirit in you, for we are all soul travelers on this journey called life. Each one of us is a temporary manifestation of the One Great Spirit that permeates all reality. We are here to bear witness and to honor the miracle of being alive; to share our gifts, to grow in awareness, and ultimately, to become conscious co-workers with God.

It is through us that the Creator wants to realize itself. As eternal beings, we exist within a dynamic interchange of energy and vibration; a great, etheric, creative Ocean of Consciousness and Love. People may refer to this ocean by many names such as God, the Creator, Source, the Universe, the Infinite Divine Spirit, or the Universal Life Force. Whatever one wants to call it, each one of us exists as a tiny droplet in this great ocean. It moves within and around us at all times and is completely accessible to assist us in all aspects of our lives. We are never separate from it, nor are we separate from each other. This is the great illusion that we must overcome.

Thoughts are energy. The Universe is always listening and responding to every energetic impulse we emit. When we send out a thought that is backed by a strong desire, feeling, or intention; we set a cause into motion, and the whole Universe collaborates to make it so. For this reason, it is important that we become conscious of our thoughts, and understand how we are all active participants in creating the reality that shows up for us. We attract into our lives exactly what we spend our time and energy thinking about. As energetic beings, we hold the power to be the architects of our reality.

The world that we see before us is a manifestation of our own consciousness. In any given moment, we can stand on the thresholds of our lives, and look out over the landscapes that we have created, shaped by our thoughts, fears, desires, emotions, and expectations.

The Universe is reflecting back to us an exact mirrored image of everything that we have ever thought about.

Within all that exists, there is a Holy Presence. This Holy Presence is the Spirit that gently guides our lives. It speaks to us through symbols and metaphors. As evolving human beings, we are being called to become aware and take notice of the guidance that is being offered. When we shift our attention away from the physical world and tune into the voice of Spirit, we begin to see everything differently. We come to understand that the events, people, and circumstances that show up in our lives, are not just random occurrences; but rather part of a great spiritual odyssey, played out on the stage of life, to open our hearts, and lead us to higher consciousness. Each one of us has a purpose and a role to play in the evolution of awareness, and the expansion of love on Earth.

# Part One
## Shattering the Great Illusion

*"You are not meant for crawling, so don't.
You have wings. Learn to use them and fly."
-Rumi*

# Chapter 1
## Floating Beyond Form

*Wait! Stop! What is happening to me?* My mind races in confusion as I scramble desperately to get my bearings. *Something is happening that I do not understand!* The last thing I remember is the babysitter tucking me into bed to go to sleep. Now, all of a sudden, I wake up to discover that I am not in my bed anymore! I am hovering weightlessly above the bed, just below the ceiling. Looking down, I can see my three-year-old body sleeping peacefully below me.

My thoughts rush to make sense of it all. *How can this be? If I am down there, sleeping on the bed, then how is it possible that I am also up here floating on the ceiling? Moreover, what am I doing on the ceiling? How did I get here?*

I quickly realize that I am no longer in my physical body. I am in a body made of light. This light body feels different than my physical body. This light body weighs nothing at all. I raise my hands out in front of me and see that they are semi-transparent, luminous, and glowing. As I glance around in disbelief, I recognize that I am not alone. My four-year-old sister, Crystal, is floating in the air beside me. She too is alarmed and shoots me a thought. *What is going on? What are we doing here?* We are both so bewildered.

*I don't know Crystal!* I reply telepathically in silence. *Here, give me your hand!*

Crystal floats closer to me and extends her hand. As I reach out to clasp her hand in mine, I am suddenly alarmed when our fingers pass right through each other. There is nothing to grasp! At that moment, I realize that we are not solid beings anymore. Crystal and

I look at each other in amazement, noticing how our bodies have changed, and how our forms are shimmering and sparkling.

Using the energetic language of thought, Crystal begins to communicate with me by sending ethereal pictures and images. To my surprise, I discover that I understand her perfectly. In silent conversation, we agree to set out and explore our surroundings in our newfound bodies of light.

Gradually, as we drift wordlessly side by side, Crystal and I begin to relax into the experience. Our confusion soon gives way to a deep sense of peace and surrender. Hovering together in complete silence, we begin to take in everything around us. We are light in the darkness. As we glance around at our surroundings, we can see the entire outline of the pale green walls of our bedroom vibrating with fluidity. I realize, in my current state of awareness, that nothing is really solid. Everything seems to be held together by vibration.

Soon Crystal and I discover that if we focus our attention together in the direction we want to go, we glide effortlessly and instantaneously toward the path of our thoughts. Making our way down the hall, we float along just below the ceiling. In our excitement, we converse with each other silently. *We're flying! We're flying!* As we grow more comfortable with our new ecstatic freedom, we practice drifting up and down the hallway together.

Eventually, after many trips back and forth through the long corridor, we both feel satisfied with our out-of-body adventure. Together, we make the decision to return to our sleeping bodies on the beds below us. The instant we direct our attention to our bodies, we are pulled back by an invisible force that eases us down gently. As Crystal and I slip back into our bodies, I feel the weight and density of my flesh form once again.

As I lay there, looking up at the ceiling, I am astounded and amazed by what just happened. *Wow! That was so much fun! We were flying! I love flying!* I think to myself happily. Yet, at the same time I wonder; *Why hasn't anybody ever told me about flying before?*

The next morning, Crystal and I wake up early and race into our mom and dad's room to tell them about our flying adventure on the ceiling. They listen halfheartedly and dismiss us casually saying, "Oh, that was just a dream. You were only dreaming!"

"No! No, that's not true!" I insist. "We were not just dreaming! It was real! I know that we were really flying together on the ceiling!"

Crystal nods her head in agreement and chimes in, "Yes! Yes! It was real! It wasn't a dream!"

Nothing my parents would ever say could change our minds about the night we flew together on the ceiling. Crystal and I know that it was not just a dream. We know for certain that it really happened. Even to this day, Crystal and I still reminisce about our mystical adventure and the night we flew free of our earthly forms.

As I look back, I realize that this incident was my first conscious, out-of-body experience. At the young age of three, my view of reality shifted and expanded abruptly. From that point forward, I've always known that it is possible to leave the body and fly and that my awareness is separate from my physical form. My perception was permanently altered and I began to see and interpret everything about the world differently. I know from my experience that even though things appear to be fixed and solid, nothing is really the way it seems. All of life is vibrating with energy and moving molecules. I discovered that by focusing my attention intently, it is possible to direct my consciousness to travel anywhere, following the direction of my thoughts. I know that in addition to having a physical body, I also have a light body that is not solid.

It would be many years before I got an explanation for what really happened on that miraculous night. In my search for the truth, I discovered ancient teachings on soul travel that validated my experience; confirming for me that in addition to having a physical body, I also have subtle bodies within my being that vibrate at higher frequencies. These subtle bodies make it possible to travel beyond the physical realm to experience different planes of consciousness. For me, this awareness changed everything.

*"The power of intuitive understanding will protect you from harm until the end of your days."*
*- Lao Tzu*

# Chapter 2
## A Child's Intuition

As a little girl, I responded to the world with heightened sensitivity. Without being told, I knew things intuitively about others. I could sense the energy fields of the people around me. In my imagination, I would step inside their bodies and feel what they were feeling. I could sense their emotions of sadness, depression, jealousy, hate, love, and joy. I could pick up on their intentions and detect whether they were being truthful with me or not. Instinctively, I knew when somebody had bad intentions or an underlying agenda, and I could discern what their motives were by paying close attention to their subtle energetic cues. For this reason, I never took things at face value. I didn't believe what people were telling me without checking in first with my innermost feelings.

When I was three and a half years old, my family moved to an isolated suburb out on the dusty plains of Littleton, Colorado. It was a new housing development just under construction, approximately fifteen miles from Denver, on a bumpy, dirt road. Our house, being one of the very first homes to be built there, sat isolated. We were surrounded by wide-open prairies, with snowcapped mountains rising in the far-off distance. At night, I would lie in my bed and listen to the coyotes howling and yipping eerily. By day, I would watch the tumbleweeds roll down the street, pushed and driven by the wind, unencumbered.

One morning in early summer, I peered out the kitchen window with an uneasy feeling. There was a strange man slowly lumbering up our driveway. I watched as his large, slouched figure shuffled up the walk like a dark shadow. He made his way bit by bit, step by step, until finally, he stood on the porch at our front door. At last, he raised his shaky, tobacco-stained fingers and rang the doorbell.

Immediately, I heard my mother's footsteps as she hurried to answer the door. I fell in behind her, tucked away in her silhouette. My mother greeted the man pleasantly from behind the screen, while I listened and watched with guarded apprehension and suspicion.

There was no doubt about it; I did not like this man. His voice was low, raspy, and gruff, and his eyes were evasive. He was heavily built and smelled of old sweat and cigarettes. As he stared at the ground, avoiding eye contact, he mumbled something about being a landscaper and said that he was doing jobs for the new homes in the neighborhood. He was wondering if our family wanted to have our yard landscaped.

It was true that our property obviously did need landscaping, so this piqued my mother's interest. Instantly, she fell into conversation with him. As this was happening, a deep feeling of uneasiness washed over me. I did not trust this man. I just knew in my heart that he was up to no good. My mind raced as they continued to talk. With each passing minute, I grew more and more impatient and agitated. The energy was boiling up inside of me and I felt the heat rushing to my face. Finally, I just couldn't take it any longer! I had to say something! Gathering up all my courage, I took a deep breath and stepped out from behind my mother's shadow. Looking up and glaring at the intrusive man directly, I blurted out, "Are you a burglar?"

A dead, awkward silence ensued. My mother was horrified and embarrassed that I should ask such a question. She feigned an apologetic smile and corrected me harshly, instructing me not to be so rude. I held my ground and stared at the man firmly and relentlessly as he stood there, noticeably shaken by my outburst. Shifting back and forth uneasily, from one foot to another, he avoided my gaze. With a nervous laugh and a forced, crooked smile, he attempted to cover his intentions. "Of course I'm not a burglar!" he struggled to assure me.

My mother ignored the incident. Even though I continued to insist that the man was a very bad man and a burglar, she hired him anyway. I learned that his name was Gene.

Given no choice in the matter, I was doomed to tolerate him as long as he was around. For the most part, I made a point to steer clear of him but kept a wary eye from a distance. Gene worked for several weeks as the summer passed; doing landscaping not only at our house but also at other newly-built homes in our neighborhood.

Finally, the day came when the last landscaping job in the neighborhood was finished and it was time for Gene to pack up and go. Alas, the man whom I had distrusted and avoided all summer, finally left town. I was so happy and relieved to be free of his disturbing, intrusive presence.

Soon after, however, there were reports of several robberies in our neighborhood. Tools were missing out of garages and building supplies had disappeared from construction sites. It also became apparent that the landscaping jobs were unprofessional and peoples' basements were flooding because of it. As things began to come to light, it became obvious that Gene was indeed a crook. He had swindled everyone in the neighborhood!

Shortly afterward, an article appeared in the local newspaper, and although I couldn't yet read, I saw Gene's picture there. It turns out that the stranger, whom I had suspected was a burglar all along, had been tracked down and arrested for theft. All of the neighbors were in shock, but I wasn't surprised at all. I said to my mother, "See! You should have believed me! I told you he was a burglar!"

This experience validated for me that I should always listen to my feelings and trust my intuition. I learned that when I get an impression about somebody, I should believe it. If something feels energetically off, I need to pay attention.

The lesson here is that there are no private thoughts. It is possible to tune in and listen telepathically to the intentions of others. Just as a pebble tossed into a pond sends out ripples over the water, thoughts go out as waves of energy traveling through the ethers. The mind is like a radio station that is constantly broadcasting and receiving messages. People who are sensitive are able to pick up on these thought forms.

    Whenever you have a gut feeling about something or someone, pay close attention to what your inner voice is telling you. Take time to tune in and listen when The Universe speaks. It whispers to guide and protect you.

*"All that we see or seem is but a dream within a dream."*
*– Edgar Allen Poe*

# Chapter 3
## The Mystery of Dreams

Have you ever wondered when you fall asleep and dream at night, which is the real reality? Is the waking world as much a dream to the dreaming world, as the dreaming world is to those awake? In truth, all of life is a dream. Whether you are sleeping or awake, messages from Spirit come in the form of symbols and metaphors. Dreams are the connection and the ongoing conversation that your soul has with the Divine.

The world of dreams is a sacred space where you can get spiritual guidance about the smallest details of your daily life. In dreams, you can commune with your angels and spirit guides to receive assistance and inspiration. You can work through problems, conflicts, and misunderstandings in your dreams, and also get clues into past lives.

Dreams provide a meeting ground for souls who reside on either side of the veil. This makes it possible to come together with long-lost loved ones, even after they have passed on. Many times, in dreams, I have reunited with family members and friends who have departed from this world. It is so heartening to have a chance to engage with them once more and check in on their well-being. I often notice that loved ones appear younger and healthier than they were before they transcended planet Earth. It is a relief for me to see that they are happy and are no longer suffering or in pain.

When you have an opportunity to connect with loved ones who have left this world, and you come to realize that they are not really gone; it is truly a gift to know that they are still with you. Even though they dwell on a different level of vibration, it is possible to reach this level in dreams. Through the Law of Attraction and a mutual desire to connect, there is an unseen force that will bring you back together again.

The land of dreams is an imperceptible world where we all journey often; however, we may not always remember our adventures there. Dreaming is a kind of "out-of-body" travel. When we go to sleep at night, consciousness is released to travel freely in the subtle realms, through many levels of awareness. The world of dreams is an invisible stage on which we play. It is a learning ground where we receive lessons, choreographed by a Higher Power, to help enrich our lives. In dreams, when our consciousness is most receptive, we often share communications with Spirit; although, in the morning when we rise, we may have no recollection of the interactions we had. Even if we can't remember, these encounters are recorded in our subconscious minds to assist us in living in attunement with our life's purpose and to guide us towards fulfilling our personal destinies.

In the realm of dreams, our thoughts manifest instantaneously. The laws of manifestation in the dream world are similar to the laws of manifestation in the material world; the only difference being that the physical world is denser and the vibrations are slower. For this reason, when a thought form goes out into the physical world, it takes longer to manifest here on the earthly plane than it takes to manifest in the subtle realm of dreams. Due to this delay, people oftentimes don't make the connection between their originating thoughts and the resulting reality they see before them.

In both the dream world and the physical world, the universal laws of cause and effect are still the same. Some people refer to this phenomenon as karma. In the dream world, when a cause is set into motion, the effect shows up instantaneously. On the earth plane, however, it may take several years before one sees the effects of events that they originally set into motion. It is easy for a person to forget what was said or done in the past, which resulted in launching a particular outcome. Whatever shows up in our lives, whether it is positive or negative, depends on the originating nature of the energy that was initially sent forth.

Most of us go through our lives never realizing that we are living a dream; and that all around us are signs and symbols from the Universe. The first step in becoming more aware of these messages from Spirit is to consciously pursue life as an active dreamer. We can start by paying close attention to all of the coincidences, random events, and the myriad of symbols and subtle metaphors that show up in our lives each day.

When you wake up enough to know that you are dreaming, something sacred occurs. Whether sleeping or awake, it is at this point that you become the "aware presence" beyond the dream. This pure awareness is the ultimate reality of your eternal self.

## Adventures in Dreaming

I was five years old, when one night, after drifting off to sleep; I awoke to find myself standing in a colorful, fragrant garden filled with pale, pink peonies, and purple iris blossoms. As I looked around me, taking it all in; I realized that I was standing in the garden located in the backyard of my childhood home. The air was soft and the atmosphere was surreal.

Glancing around, I saw my sister, Crystal, standing nearby on a green, grassy hill. She was wearing her favorite red shorts and a white t-shirt. Her shoulder-length, tousled, blond hair glistened in the sun as she tilted her head sideways. In one hand she held a small, yellow, plastic shovel and in the other, she swung a bright, blue bucket. Upon seeing me standing there, Crystal skipped towards me happily and shouted. "Hey, Sharon! Do you want to plant a garden?"

"Sure!" I said with excitement. "Let's plant it over here, next to the fence, by these pretty, purple irises."

We knelt down together and started to clear out the dried grasses, uncovering a patch of dirt where our garden would grow. Crystal took her shovel in hand and began to dig the earth. "I'm going to plant peas!" she said joyfully, as she threw dirt in every direction.

Immediately, my mood changed drastically; for if there was one thing I couldn't stand, it was peas!

"Peas?" I said with alarm, "Oh no, not peas!" I begged. "No!" I said defiantly. "I don't like peas! I don't want any peas in the garden! I want to plant carrots!"

As we bantered back and forth in the dream, about whether we should plants peas or carrots, I suddenly felt very uncomfortable in my physical body. The discomfort jolted me out of the dream. My body was hot, cold, and shivering, all at the same time. As it turned out, I was running a very high fever. I woke up and began to cry.

My father heard me from the next room and came in to console me. He picked me up out of bed and held me while I sobbed. "Why are you crying, Cheri?" he asked, addressing me lovingly by my nickname.

Before I could open my mouth to answer, Crystal sat upright in bed and interjected, "I know why she is crying! It's because she doesn't want me to plant peas in the garden. She wants to plant carrots! But Daddy, it's okay; Sharon can plant carrots in the garden if she wants to. I won't plant any peas."

All at once, I realized that something remarkable had happened. Crystal and I had been sharing the same dream!

"No Crystal," I answered. "I know what you mean, but that's not why I am crying. I'm crying because I don't feel well."

My father was stumped. He had no idea what we were talking about, however, at that moment, Crystal and I had an epiphany. We both knew that the dream we had shared was more than just a fantasy. We gained an understanding that the world of dreams is a realm in which we can actively participate and share experiences.

This event confirmed the validity of the dream world and illustrated to me that on some level, the experiences that we have in dreams while sleeping, are as valid as those experiences that we have when we are awake. Since that time, I have always paid close attention to my dreams.

As I grew older, I began to keep a dream journal. In doing so, I discovered that my dreams where oftentimes prophetic. I would know when somebody, who lived far away, was struggling with an illness and hiding it from others. Sometimes, I would have a dream that a person close to me would soon be leaving this world. I became conscious of the fact that in my dreams, I was frequently foreseeing events before they happened. Occasionally, I would have a dream that was particularly disturbing and it would bother me greatly; for I anticipated that at some point down the road, that dream might very well come to pass.

Once, I had a dream that troubled me for years. I dreamt that I was a passenger in a car, being driven on an underpass that was surrounded by concrete barriers. Suddenly there was an earthquake! The road and cement guardrails started cracking and crashing down all around us. The car I was in, jolted sharply to one side, dropped into a hole, and became stuck. We were trapped! I awoke in the middle of the dream feeling terrified and never knew exactly how the dream turned out in the end.

The dream was frightening and haunted me for years. Due to my previous experiences with prophetic dreams, I was dreading the day that this dream might come true. I felt apprehension about going to earthquake-prone areas, and I was always on the lookout for anything that resembled the particular underpass I had seen in my dream.

Well, as I had anticipated, the day finally came when my dreaded dream did come true; although, it didn't quite happen in the way I had expected. Thirty years had passed since I had the initial dream about the earthquake. I was visiting "Universal Studios" in California, taking a tour of the back lots and the movie sets where everything was staged and filmed. As we were being driven around by a tour guide in an open taxi, all at once, we entered an area that looked exactly like the setting I had seen in my haunting dream. We came to an underpass. There were concrete barriers on both sides and concrete above us as well. Suddenly, the road started shaking back and forth, and the vehicle lurched to and fro. The road began to crack all around us as the car lunged sideways, dropping into a hole. We were stuck!

As all of this was unfolding, I realized at that moment that my dreaded dream had finally come true! I laughed to myself with a sigh of relief. The joke was on me! This situation that I had dreamt about, and feared for at least thirty years; turned out to be nothing more than a simulated earthquake, staged for a movie set at Universal Studios in Hollywood!

In any case, it is important to pay close attention to your dreams. A message may present itself in a number of ways. As you learn to be an active dreamer, set the intention to remain awake and aware in consciousness while dreaming. You may also want to keep a dream journal. With practice, you will get better and better at deciphering the language of your dreams.

You can make a request to receive guidance in your dreams about any particular issue that you are dealing with. Write down your questions in your journal before you go to sleep. In the morning, you may notice that something has shifted. Even though you might not remember your dream, you may wake up with clarity about a situation that's been bothering you. It could be that suddenly you know exactly what needs to be done in order to solve your problem. Working with your dreams can provide you with an easy and natural way to receive spiritual insight and guidance on your journey through life.

*"Imagination is the only weapon
in the war against reality"
- Jules De Gaultier*

# Chapter 4
## Lessons in Creating Reality

I was nineteen years old when my mother asked if I would like to attend a four-day seminar in Denver called "Silva Mind Control". She said that it was a seminar about learning to master the mind, based on the world-famous mind techniques developed by Jose Silva. My mother explained to me that in this seminar, I would learn to use the power of my mind to achieve my goals and dreams. I would be trained to develop my psychic abilities, and would be educated in self-hypnosis along with other skills that would help me to improve my memory and expand my mental power.

Everything that my mother told me about Silva Mind Control sounded very interesting to me. In a way, it seemed too good to be true; but if it was true, the thought of being able to take control of my mind to create the world of my dreams, was something I really wanted to learn. I agreed to go to with her and explore what it was all about. When I made the decision to attend the seminar, I had no idea that it would be a major turning point in my life. I was about to embark upon a journey that would throw open the doors of my limited consciousness and teach me to tap into the infinite power of the Universe.

On the day of the seminar, my mother and I chatted in the car with enthusiasm as we drove to Denver, unaware of how our lives were about to change. We arrived early and watched as a crowd of people gathered in the large hotel conference room. I noticed that I seemed to be the youngest attendee there. There were folks from all walks of life: people seeking healing, housewives, businessmen, doctors, nurses, coaches, students, and athletes. Some people were sitting in chairs placed against the wall, but most of the attendees were seated on the floor in the center of the large, sprawling room. My mother and I chose to take our place on the floor. We settled in, sitting cross-legged on the paisley red and gold carpet, and waited excitedly in anticipation for the program to begin. Before long, a tall, graceful woman, dressed in professional attire, picked up a microphone and began to speak in a warm, relaxed manner.

The instructor welcomed us all, explaining that she would be teaching us how to access and use a greater portion of our brains. She went on to explain that science has proven that our brains emit electrical impulses that can be identified with different states of consciousness. These electrical impulses can be measured in pulses per second. The calculated rate of vibration is referred to as "brain wave frequency". She told us that we would be learning to consciously slow down our brain waves in order to access a level of mind called, "the alpha state". She went on to explain that it is from this state of mind that we would be able to gain control of the subconscious mind and access the spiritual dimension.

Over the course of the next four days, we were guided through numerous meditative exercises. We were taught that the mental screen of the mind, also known in mysticism as "the third eye" or the "seat of the soul", is a blank canvas on which we can project mental images to create anything we desire. It can be accessed when we close our eyes and focus our attention on the inner point between the eyebrows. We were told that everything begins as a thought before it materializes, and that mental pictures act as a spiritual blueprint to manifest form.

As a class, we practiced slowing down our brain waves, in order to attain the alpha state of consciousness at will. Once we were able to do this, we worked on increasing our powers of visualization by projecting colors and numbers onto the mental screens of our minds. As we all became more proficient in the mind control exercises, we began to understand that mastering control of visualization and imagination is an energy gathering process that can be used to create change in our lives. We gained an awareness of how we are constantly creating our own personal realities with every positive or negative thought, and how important it is for us to be the guardians at the gates of our minds, allowing only beneficial energies and thoughts to enter.

In order to uncover and experience our hidden powers of clairvoyance; we practiced techniques for projecting our consciousness to other places and gathering information psychically. We studied human anatomy charts to develop a reference for using clear mental pictures in visualizations and psychic healing. We learned to sharpen our telepathic skills, by sending and receiving mental images with other participants in the class.

At the end of the seminar, we were told that in order to become a graduate of Silva Mind Control, we were required to pass a final exam. This would be a test of our abilities to perform psychic diagnosis and healing. To begin, we were each asked to write down, on a small piece of paper, the name and location of a person who needed healing, along with the ailment that they were suffering from. As the instructor collected the bits of paper in a hat, mixing and shuffling them together, I felt anxious about my abilities to pass the test.

One by one we were called to the center of the room. For each student, the instructor pulled a piece of paper from the hat and read the name and location of the person who was in need of healing. The student was then asked to take a moment to slow down their brain waves and to access the alpha state of mind. Next, they were instructed to project an image of the person onto the mental screen of their mind and to scan every aspect of that person's anatomy; looking for areas of weakness. The student was requested to report their findings to the instructor and then to send appropriate visualizations and images to assist in healing.

When my turn came, I made my way shyly to the center of the room, feeling apprehensive as I reached into the hat, pulled out a scrap of paper, and handed it to the instructor. She read me a man's name and his location, which was somewhere in South Carolina. I closed my eyes and went into meditation; slowing down my brain waves to attain the alpha state of consciousness. Then, when I felt ready, I projected the man's image onto my inner mental screen. The first thing I noticed about him was that he was very unstable on his feet. In my mind's eye, he was loose and limp and he kept falling down. I reported this to the instructor. In this exam, I was requested to describe everything exactly as I saw it and not to judge anything intellectually. I then began to mentally scan his body and conveyed to the instructor that I saw a dark cloud covering his liver, and also sensed that this man was struggling with overwhelming feelings of sadness and hopelessness.

Upon relaying what I was seeing and feeling, the instructor nodded, indicating that my findings were correct. She then told me to proceed with the session by sending healing energy to this man. I used my imagination to clear and disburse the cloud over his liver and flooded the area with white light to dispel the darkness. I imagined his liver to be healthy and vibrant. Then, I steadied the man from repeatedly falling down, by lifting him up mentally and holding him upright, imagining that he was strong and grounded, like a tree. I surrounded him in an aura of pink glowing light, the color of love and compassion. When I was finished with the healing, I ended the session with the affirmation, "So Be It".

After I concluded the session, the instructor validated my findings. The man was an alcoholic. That explained why, in my vision, he was having such a hard time standing. He was also suffering from cirrhosis of the liver; which had been indicated in my mind's eye as a dark cloud over the liver. The man was facing feelings of hopelessness and despair due to his condition. I had picked up on everything correctly.

With this validation, not only did I surprise myself, but I had officially passed the exam in psychic healing. I became a graduate of Silva Mind Control. From that day forward, my whole perspective and my approach to life changed completely. I began to integrate everything I learned at the seminar into every aspect of my life. A whole new world had opened up for me. With the training I received in Silva Mind Control; many of my early childhood, psychic experiences were validated and I began to understand more about the workings of the inner worlds. Just as I had suspected as a little girl, I received confirmation that consciousness does exist outside the body. It is possible to travel beyond the flesh to gather information and to have true experiences. I learned to become acutely aware that with every thought and intention, I construct my reality and it is my responsibility to be the master of my mind and the architect of my life.

*"Make yourself familiar with the Angels, and behold them frequently in spirit. Without being seen, they are present with you."*
-St. Francis de Sales

# Chapter 5

## Angelic Intervention

It was the dark of the moon on Halloween night in 1978. I was twenty-two years old, living in the mountains near the old mining town of Gold Hill, Colorado. My best friend, Athena, and I shared an A-frame cabin that was surrounded by wildflower meadows and the high country peaks of the Continental Divide. We were like sisters and did just about everything together. On this night, we had great plans to celebrate Halloween, the ancient Celtic Festival of Samhain. There were several parties to attend on our agenda, and we were both joyfully anticipating a full night of festivities.

We laughed and giggled light-heartedly as we shuffled through a pile of colorful vintage clothing and odd, random accessories; looking for the perfect items to embellish our costumes. Athena had adorned herself in a soft, buff-colored suede dress, complete with fringe and matching moccasins. I watched as she wove white feathers into her thick, black hair that spilled in waves over her shoulders. She turned and looked at me smiling, with bright emerald eyes and her usual impish grin. Finally, she was ready; pleased with her transformation into an Indian princess.

I was dressed as an angel in a swirly, pink skirt and a white, chiffon blouse with flutter sleeves. To complete my costume, I placed a garland of dried rosebuds into my curly, blond hair and strapped a pair of iridescent angel wings onto my back. Athena and I stood before the mirror and looked at ourselves with satisfaction. Then, merrily we set off for a night of fun and adventure.

As we stepped outside into the cool autumn air, we could see that our good friends, Bjarne and Peter, were waiting for us. Bjarne was tall, with pale-blond, shoulder-length hair and captivating blue eyes. I could see as he approached that he was dressed in a long black coat. I studied his face with amusement. There was a black vertical line running from the top of his forehead down to his chin that divided his face into two parts. One side of his face was painted blue and the other half was yellow. I examined his costume with curiosity, noticing that he appeared to be a funny conglomeration of opposites. He had a black circle around one eye and a white circle around the other. Somehow he had managed to coax his flaxen hair to stand up stiff and straight on one side, while on the other side, it draped loosely over his shoulder. One corner of his mouth was painted into a smile, and the opposite side turned down into a frown.

I stood there looking at him in confusion. Finally, I asked with curiosity, "What or who are you supposed to be?"

Bjarne broke into a pleased grin and answered, "You can call me, Part Two!"

Peter stood beside Bjarne. He was tall and thin, with curly red hair and freckles that danced across his nose. Dressed as a clown, he wore a massive, multi-colored wig, which underneath it all, made him look a bit gangly. His brown, shining eyes were painted like stars.

Peter volunteered to be the chosen driver. We all crammed into his blue VW Bug and drove into the setting sun. Bouncing over rocks and kicking up large clouds of thick, brown dust, we made our way down the mountain. We were headed for a party at a cabin in Four Mile Canyon, near a mining town called Wall Street. After driving several miles, we diverted from the main road and came to a very narrow, rocky road that led to our destination. Not wanting to negotiate the treacherous dirt road on the way back up the mountain after dark, we made the decision to park the car at a small pullover and walk the rest of the way to the party.

As I stepped out of the cramped car, straightened up, and stretched my arms to the sky, I took a deep breath. The forest was dressed in golden hues, and the crisp autumn wind clattered the dried foliage in the changing aspen trees. The leaves fell gently to the ground, one by one, landing in a carpet of red, yellow, and gold. The sun cast long shadows, spreading a warm amber light across the land.

We all set out to hike up the 4-wheel drive road that led to the party. As we walked, we were excited and energized, for this was Halloween night; the night when the veil between the physical world and the spirit world is believed to be the thinnest. A sense of mystery and magic filled the air and it felt as though almost anything could happen.

After walking just a short distance, we came upon a dark, ominous hole in the ground. We all stopped abruptly in disbelief. There, before us, was an uncovered, abandoned mineshaft, looming in the fading light at the edge of the road. It was a ghostly remnant from the past; one of the many open mineshafts still found in the mountains around Boulder today. The hole was large enough for a car to fall into, and there were no fences or signs to warn people of the impending danger.

As we all peered eerily over the edge of the dark abyss, my stomach leapt to my throat. "Whoa! I wouldn't want to fall down there!" I said, feeling suddenly very queasy.

"Me neither!" Athena, Bjarne, and Peter all chimed in unison. We backed away from the hole with trepidation and continued on our way.

When we finally arrived at the party, we entered an open, expansive room that had been set up for dancing. It was decorated with orange, glowing jack-o-lanterns, and large, cardboard cutouts of witches, spiders, and goblins, pasted on the walls. In one corner, there was a DJ playing records on a turntable. Dressed as a ghost in a flapping white sheet, he bobbed his head up and down to the rhythm of the beat. I laughed with amusement as I watched all of the costumed characters on the dance floor, grooving to the music.

Adjacent to the dance hall, there was a room darkened with black sheets that had been turned into a haunted chamber.

Bjarne, Peter, Athena, and I danced together, enjoyed some Halloween treats and made our way spookily through the haunted house. After a couple of hours, we all decided it was time to move on. The night was still young and we had other parties to attend.

We left the party feeling jovial, accompanied by other ghouls, goblins, witches, and fairies. Slowly we picked our way back down the rocky dirt road. We could barely see a thing, and none of us had remembered to bring a flashlight. Athena, Bjarne, and Peter all walked ahead of me, while I fell behind, chatting with a young man who was dressed as Dracula. In spite of the darkness, I could see that he was clothed in black and wore a short wig of tangled, dark hair. His face was painted with black circles around his eyes, and his lips wore a ruby red frown.

As we tentatively picked our way through the darkness, all of a sudden, a black colored Jeep came skidding around the corner, heading straight towards us! I was blinded abruptly by the oncoming headlights and stepped off the road quickly to get out of the way. All at once, the ground disappeared from under my feet and a sobering fear washed over me. My heart sank in absolute terror as I realized that I was falling... free falling in darkness!

*Oh!* I thought to myself as I faced my fate, *I must be dying now!* My mind raced as I tried to put together what was happening. In my haste to get out of the way of the oncoming car, I figured that I must have stepped off the edge of the open mineshaft that we had all seen on our way to the party. As I continued to plummet through obscurity in horror, everything took on a surreal quality. It felt like I was falling in slow motion. A sense of calm enveloped me, as I realized that there was nothing I could do, but surrender to the experience.

It seemed like I had been falling for eternity when at last, I landed lightly on my feet. It felt like an angel had been supporting me from underneath and gently set me down. I was elated to discover that I had survived the fall! I was still alive! Looking around me, I saw nothing but darkness as I attempted to assess my situation.

All at once, I heard a concerned voice calling uneasily from above, "Are you okay?"

I recognized that voice. It was Dracula. I answered feebly, somewhat in a state of shock. "Yes, I'm okay. I think I'm okay."

Dracula shouted, "I'm coming down after you!"

"No!" I said. "Stay where you are!" I didn't want him to take the risk. "Please don't come down here! Please, just go get help! I don't want you to hurt yourself!" I pleaded.

Dracula didn't listen and proceeded to climb down the jagged pieces of metal that were sticking out from the center of the mine. I could hear him grunting and breathing hard, as he made his way down to where I was standing. At last, he heard my voice next to him. In total darkness, he assumed that upon hearing my voice, he must be close to the bottom of the mineshaft. With his legs dangling freely, he let go of the metal he was hanging onto; figuring that it was only a short hop to reach the ground. Unfortunately, he was wrong. Upon letting go, he became instantly airborne and began falling too, tumbling even further into the bleak abyss. There was a long, painful silence... until at last, I heard him land with a loud yell.

"Are you okay?" I asked, waiting nervously for a reply.

A weak, uncertain voice answered me, "I think so."

At that point, Dracula suggested that he light a match, so we could both see our surroundings. I had heard that gases can accumulate in mines, and I worried that lighting a match could cause an explosion. Although I tried to protest, he lit a match anyway. Thankfully, we didn't explode! Instead, we surveyed the miracle of our survival.

Looking around in the dim light, I discovered that I was standing on a small wooden shelf, approximately one-square-foot in size. It was precariously attached to the unstable wall of the mineshaft with two tiny wooden braces. I guessed that the rickety shelf had been used to set buckets on, by the miners who had worked in the mine.

For me, however, this little shelf was my lifeline. I was amazed that it was even supporting my weight.

Marveling at how I had landed so accurately and precisely, I seemed to be unharmed except for some minor cuts on my stomach. If I had landed differently, or moved my foot an inch or two in either direction; I would have most certainly lost my balance and fallen to my death. As I gazed down at my angel costume, I contemplated the profundity of the fact that I was still alive. It all seemed like a dream.

Through the murky darkness, I could see Dracula standing below me at the bottom of the mineshaft. To my amazement, he was also unharmed. He had landed safely in a clear area that was otherwise surrounded by sharp, twisted metal debris. He didn't have a scratch on him.

Dracula looked up and saw me standing on the small wooden shelf. "I'm coming up!" he announced boldly.

Jumping as high as he could, he grabbed hold of the metal above him and began his climb up to where I was. When he was finally beside me, he straddled his way over to join me on the fragile shelf.

Suddenly, there was a sharp, crackling crack and the shelf began to break away from the crumbling wall! A sense of doom washed over us as we felt the shelf begin to give way under our combined weight. I started to panic, wondering what was going to happen next. *Was it possible that we were going to fall to our deaths after all?*

At that very second, I looked up and saw the glare of a car's headlights shining above us. Miraculously, there was a cable being lowered from a winch and it was almost within my grasp. In another second, just as the shelf was breaking away, Dracula and I grabbed onto the cable, and in the knick-of-time, we were lifted to safety.

Once again, we were standing on solid ground, overjoyed to finally be out of that chilling, black dungeon! With a huge sigh of relief, we gave each other a hug. At last, the ordeal was over. We were safe and alive!

Later, I found out that the man, who rescued us, was the same man who had been driving the Jeep that forced me off the road in the first place. The mine was on his property. He had seen me step out of the way and knew that I had disappeared down the mineshaft.

Hurriedly, I made my way back down the mountain to where the car had been parked; figuring that Athena, Bjarne, and Peter must be tired of waiting for me. When I got there, however, I discovered that the car was gone and they had left without me. They thought I had most likely changed my mind about leaving and had gone back to the party. They figured I would catch a ride with other friends.

I turned around and made my way back up the road, this time making sure to steer clear of the mineshaft. When I arrived back at the party, I entered the dance hall once again, feeling ecstatic! I was alive! I danced with joy; so grateful for my life, so grateful for the moment. I was only vaguely aware of the flurry of people all around me who were whispering to each other, "Did you hear about the girl who fell down the mineshaft?"

Nobody suspected it was me. I had only a few hidden scratches on my stomach. I had been saved. My life had been spared. I knew with absolute certainty that I had been protected, carried gently in the arms of angels!

This experience assured me that there is a purpose for my life and a reason for my survival. My journey is still unfolding. I don't really think of angels as beings with wings and halos, but rather as a loving, protective presence that surrounds me at all times. Since this experience, I have become acutely aware that there are always angels by my side. I call upon them often, for help in matters big and small. They shine their light into all areas of my life to illuminate my way and open my heart.

*"Life and death are one, even as the river and sea are one."*
*-Kahlil Gibran*

# Chapter 6
## Between Worlds

As I have said many times before, consciousness is eternal. It exists independently of the body. When the body dies, consciousness lives on as awareness, no longer tethered to the flesh. Although consciousness is able to travel anywhere at any time with lightning speed; in our everyday lives, we tend to focus our consciousness in our bodies. This creates the illusion that we <u>are</u> our bodies and so, we come to identify ourselves and validate our existence through physical form.

Over the years, I have had many glimpses into what it feels like to be free of the body while remaining totally conscious. One incident, in particular, was a profound out-of-body experience that happened to me while I was in the dentist's chair.

It was a hot, summer day in July when I arrived at the dentist's office to have a number of fillings replaced on one side of my mouth. I knew it was going to be a long procedure and I was somewhat apprehensive. I was escorted into the room and instructed to lie down in the reclining dentist's chair. As I laid there waiting, I squirmed and squinted nervously into the bright light overhead. Finally, a young, pleasant woman with short, blond hair and a perfect smile entered the room. She greeted me cordially and sat down on a low stool next to me, to examine my mouth. She seemed kind as she discussed the procedure that I was about to undergo. Her voice was soothing, confident, and gentle as she suggested giving me nitrous oxide sedation to make me feel more comfortable. I had never been administered nitrous oxide before, but I trusted her judgment and agreed to give it a try.

The dentist stepped out of the room and instructed the young dental assistant, who was standing nearby, to prepare me for the procedure. The assistant entered the room, dressed in a crisp, white uniform. She smiled sweetly as she placed a mask over my mouth and nose. As I recall, she told me to breathe deeply as she reached down to turn a nearby valve to the "on" position. She then walked away and went about her business of gathering and preparing the dental tools that were to be used for the procedure.

The instant I began to breathe in the gas, I was abruptly launched out of my body! Suddenly, I found myself looking down from the ceiling. I recognized instantly that this was reminiscent of the experience I had back when I was three years old; when my sister and I traveled out of our bodies. Once again, I had the realization that I was not my body, but rather, I was conscious awareness hovering in space. Looking down from my perspective just below the ceiling, I could view everything that was happening. The walls that divided the separate rooms from each other disappeared completely. From my vantage point, I could see every person who was in the building all at once. I was also aware of everybody's thoughts. Instantly, I knew what each and every person was thinking. I was especially aware of the negative and resentful feelings in the air; the suppressed animosities that people were holding against each other. Energetically, I realized that it was a very toxic environment.

As I was observing all that was going on from my place on the ceiling, eventually, the dentist entered the room to begin the procedure. She sat down next to me and began to fiddle with her instruments. I watched from above as she leaned over and began to ask me some trivial questions, just to make conversation.

"Hello, Sharon. Is your mouth beginning to feel numb yet?" she inquired.

I could see her from my elevated viewpoint on the ceiling, and I could hear her clearly; but when I tried to answer her question,

I discovered that no matter how hard I tried, it was impossible for me to move my mouth to utter a word. I realized then that I was also unable to get my body to respond to my attempts to make it move. I felt completely detached from my body, which seemed to be paralyzed.

Suddenly, the dentist grew very alarmed. She began to tap me on the cheek, saying my name very loudly over and over; "Sharon, Sharon, Wake up!"

Once again, I tried to respond, but no matter how hard I tried, I couldn't animate my mouth to form any words to speak. I wanted to tell her that I was okay. I knew I was okay. It actually struck me as somewhat funny. There I was, watching everything from the ceiling and nobody could see me. It felt a little like I was playing a game of hide-and-seek.

Eventually, the dentist eyed the valves on the nitrous oxide gas tank. She reached over abruptly and turned the valve to "off". At that moment, I was immediately propelled back into my body. Apparently, something had gone wrong and there wasn't enough oxygen mixing with the nitrous gas. Once I was back in my body again, I was able to inform the dentist that I was okay. All was well and she was able to finish the procedure without further complications.

When I walked out of the dentist's office though, I was not the same as when I walked in. I knew that I would not be able to drive home yet, so I set out for a stroll. As I made my way down the street, I realized that I was still in a heightened state of awareness. Everything was different. Nothing seemed to be solid. The colors were bright and vivid and everything was vibrating around me. I felt the life and consciousness of the trees and the grasses. As I passed people on the street, I realized that there were no secret thoughts. I could instantly detect their emotional state and was keenly aware of their joys and sorrows. Everything I was experiencing was with expanded awareness.

This incident reminded me of the lessons I had learned as a child; that nothing is really solid and everything is vibrating with life. It gave me even further validation that consciousness is fully aware and free of limitations. I felt as though I had been suspended on the border between the physical world and the ethereal worlds. This experience reassured me, with absolute certainty, that there is nothing to fear when we leave the body in death. Our souls continue to live on as conscious awareness.

*"Thus all things altered. Nothing dies. And here and there the unbodied spirit flies"* -Ovid

# Chapter 7
## Corridors of Time

It was a dismal, cold day in February when I got the news that my beloved friend, Dave, had passed from this world unexpectedly. Dave was an extremely talented guitar player, who had played in several bands around Boulder, in the 1980s and early 1990s. He was tall and thin, with a soft, gentle presence, and flowing, blond hair.

Dave and my husband, Joe, played in a band together. They shared a deep, intuitive connection that was especially apparent when they played music. Sometimes, I would accompany them when they toured and performed in the different ski towns around Colorado. Frequently, after a performance, we would stay overnight in a condominium provided by the venue. During these times, Joe, Dave, and I would stay up all night talking; sharing stimulating conversations about spiritual matters. This would go on until the wee hours of the morning when at last we would see the sun peeking up over the mountains.

Dave was an extremely kind, warm, and sensitive person. Unfortunately, however, he also frequently battled depression. One day, in the depths of despair, he ended his own life. When I first heard about Dave's passing, I was devastated. It was impossible for me to believe that I would never see him again in the physical form. I thought back to our conversations and felt comforted as I recollected the discussions we'd had about life, death, and the eternal survival of the soul. I felt certain that although Dave was gone from this earth plane, his spirit would live on forever and somehow we would meet again.

Two nights after Dave's passing, he came to me in a dream. I awoke suddenly, aware that I was outside of my physical body, standing next to him in my subtle body. He communicated with me silently and indicated that he wanted to take me on a journey, to show me something wonderful. I hesitated for just a second and then agreed to come. In that instant, I felt myself being lifted weightlessly. The next thing I knew, we were moving like ghosts through the ethers, picking up speed as we went. At last, we came upon a clearing that opened up to a mountainous landscape.

As I stood there taking it all in; all of a sudden, Dave disappeared and then re-appeared instantaneously on a craggy mountaintop above me. His tall silhouette stood victorious, as his fair hair glistened in the sun and moved with the wind. He reminded me of a great wizard, standing strong in his glory. Dave gazed at me with piercing, blue eyes. Reaching out his hand, he smiled and motioned for me to follow him. He wanted to show me the worlds beyond death.

Initially, I was astonished to see Dave alive and so full of vigor, after I had been grieving his death over the past couple of days. I accepted this new reality, however, and reached up to take his hand. Immediately, we were whisked away and I felt myself being propelled through a tunnel, like the rushing wind. I heard a whooshing sound as an unseen force pulled us along. The walls of the tunnel were composed of swirling, iridescent lights that were more energetic than solid. Before long, we arrived on the other side.

As we emerged from the tunnel, the first thing I noticed was an all-encompassing light. It was soft, glowing, and comforting; made up of warm colors like pale pink, peach, and glistening gold. I looked around and saw that we were alone. As we stood together in a great, white marble hallway, I noticed that there were multitudes of arched doorways lined up on both sides, stretching into infinity.

Dave smiled and motioned for me to enter the first doorway with him. As we moved together under the archway, I had no idea that as we crossed over the threshold, we were entering a portal in time. Emerging out on the other side, I found myself standing in my childhood home. My beloved dog, Ginger, was there to greet me; jumping and wagging her tail excitedly. I was ecstatic to see her again! Stroking her floppy, golden ears, I kissed her on the forehead and gazed once again into her soft brown eyes.

Standing in the kitchen where my family used to gather, I turned around slowly to take in my surroundings. Nothing had changed. To me, it felt like I had merely gone on a trip and was just returning home, after a long absence. I ran my hands over the chipped, black wooden chairs that still needed painting and the black metal table, where I used to sit every night and eat dinner with my siblings. Everything was exactly as I remembered.

I made my way to my brothers' bedroom and saw Peter and Stevie, sitting together on the floor. They were playing a game, arguing back and forth, just like they always used to do, about whose turn it was to go next. I stood there as an observer watching them, reliving old memories. They were completely unaware of my presence. After a time, Dave motioned for me to follow him further. We made our way back through the archway, and once again, we found ourselves standing in the long, marble corridor.

Dave and I floated along together easily. Going from doorway to doorway, we moved in and out through several different portals in time. Through one doorway, I saw my best friend, Janette, and her horse, Lucky. Janette and I had spent many happy days in our childhood years, riding together on Lucky's back. It was one of my favorite memories. I reflected on how wonderful it is to know that we can revisit past times; that on some level, these times still exist and we can return to them. Nothing is ever really lost.

Dave continued to accompany me and be my guide as we drifted in and out of the arched doorways. I was so excited and having so much fun that I didn't want to stop! In my newfound freedom, I yearned to explore everything and go everywhere. Soon, I got carried away. I made the decision that I didn't want to return back to Earth. I became obstinate and was no longer willing to stay with my guide.

I began playing hide-and-seek, racing through the corridors of time, evading all of Dave's efforts to call me back.

Alas, Dave finally had to step in to take control of the situation. He had to insist that I go back to my physical body. I indicated to him that I didn't intend to obey him. I wanted to keep going. At that point, Dave grew ten times in size, standing tall and majestic before me. His eyes, like blue lasers of light, pierced through me as he pointed his finger in my direction. I had no choice. Instantly, I found myself catapulting back through the tunnel, hurling through space, back to Earth. It felt as though I was being sucked through a huge vacuum. Racing with incredible speed, I began to worry about how I was going to land. My concerns were quickly appeased, however, when suddenly I landed, light as a feather; easing back gently into my sleeping body on the bed. I realized at that moment there is nothing to fear. Soul has no weight at all. It's impossible to get injured.

As I lay there in my bed, grappling with reality and trying to make sense of what had just happened; I looked over at my husband, Joe, sleeping peacefully beside me. I smiled as I thought to myself, "He would never, ever believe where I have been; never in a million years!"

I let my head settle deep into the pillow, feeling as though everything had changed. I had discovered a huge secret. Nothing in time is lost. In truth, time is an illusion. All of the past events of our lives still exist and are happening on some level, simultaneously. We can still go back and have those conversations that we wished we'd had. We can still correct the errors of the past.

This adventure of traveling in time has never left me. It remains with me to this day as one of the most profound, life-altering experiences I've ever had, waking or sleeping. It assured me that we are eternal beings who dwell timelessly in multiple dimensions. Death is nothing to fear.

*"Until one has loved an animal, a part of one's soul remains unawakened."* -Anatole France

# Chapter 8
## Animal Soul Friends

Animals are my world. There is something about being in the presence of animals that touches a place deep within my heart and fills my life with meaning. Every morning, as I lie in bed, watching the sun spread brilliant rays of amber, pink, and gold over the mountains; the ravens fly in from far and wide to gather in the trees outside my window. They know where I sleep; and they watch me from their perches in the pine trees, waiting impatiently while I drink my coffee leisurely.

At last, I roll out of bed lazily and step out onto the balcony to survey the scene. Looking below me, I see a mama moose lying peacefully in the snowfield with her two young calves. As I make my way downstairs, accompanied by my three dogs Déjà, Starla, and Copper, I can hear the birds' calls growing louder and louder. I pull back the curtains to a sudden flurry of fluttering wings, as I am greeted enthusiastically by my wild feathered friends.

After filling my pail with birdseed, I step outside. The cawing of the crows echoes through the crisp mountain air, as the ravens dive and greet me, flying in circles above my head. Their flapping wings make a whooshing sound as they dash through the air. It has become their morning ritual.

There are also magpies, pigeons, stellar jays, wild turkeys and a myriad of other birds waiting for me. A rabbit scurries by quickly to hide in the woodpile. In the distance, I can see my fox friend, Mystic, playing with her young kits in the meadow. At the same time, my two kitties, Rusty and Jakey, peer at me through the window. This is my life. I am always happiest when I am surrounded by animals. It is a blessing to live in a mountain sanctuary where there is abundant wildlife around me.

From the time I was a small child, I have had a deep connection with animals. Instinctively, I've always felt that it was my duty to take care of them and to watch out for their well-being. I have come to appreciate that animals are kindred souls with consciousness. They travel the path of life with us and are here on Earth for a reason. They enrich our existence and help us in many ways.

I don't believe that animals are lesser beings than humans; but rather, they are equipped with different attributes, uniquely suited to help them survive the conditions they face on Earth. They deserve our utmost respect and compassion. While humans depend on intellect and the ability to manipulate the environment in order to survive comfortably, the animals draw from ancestral memories, heightened sensitivity, and intuition. They use telepathy, subtle body movements, and vocal cues to communicate with each other. Animals have rich emotional lives and complicated family relationships.

There are countless forms that a soul may choose to inhabit on this planet. No matter what the physical form may look like; it is the internal soul consciousness, the Divine spark within, which animates the flesh and has value. Each distinctive form offers a different experience and a unique perspective that will help to further that particular soul's growth. The souls of animals are on a journey to grow and develop through earthly experiences, in the same way that our own souls are destined to evolve. We can help our animal friends to grow in consciousness, just as they can help us.

The relationships that we share with animals can be deeply profound. I believe that just as we are destined to have certain people in our lives, we are also pre-destined to share our lives with certain animals. Oftentimes, there is something mysterious and miraculous about the way an animal appears in our lives. An animal may show up as a stray, or there may be a series of coincidences that serve to bring an animal and a person together. Sometimes, an animal comes to us to offer emotional support, just when we need it most.

Animals merge energetically with the people they are with. For this reason, it is important to be mindful of the energy we exude when we are around them. Animals keep us honest. They absorb our energy and mirror it back to us. If an animal is acting aggressive or agitated; oftentimes, it is a manifestation of the energy they have accumulated from the environment and the people around them. Animals don't pretend. They are keen observers and see us for who we are. At times, they seem to know us better than we know ourselves. Animals are highly perceptive, emotionally intelligent individuals who become attuned to the subtleties of our own actions. Our animal friends can sense our energy and relate to us on a deep emotional level. They can tell when we are depressed, worried, happy, excited, anxious, or afraid.

If you have ever been lucky enough to share a special friendship with an animal, then you know that there is a sacred bond of love that transcends all boundaries. The animal companions in your life become energetic extensions of who you are. The bond is intertwining on many levels.

There is a strong interconnection between a person's physical and emotional well-being and the health and well-being of their companion animal. An animal's issues are often a reflection of their guardian's own physical or emotional issues. When a person and an animal share a deep connection, they can help to heal each other.

Throughout my lifetime, I have been blessed to have many close friendships with animals; including dogs, cats, horses, foxes, birds, rabbits, a monkey, and even a baby jaguar. Animals come into our lives for many reasons. They appear just when we need them most; as friends, guides, teachers, healers, and as angels to protect us. They come disguised as fur and flesh, offering pure, unconditional love. Their mission on Earth is to awaken our hearts.

*"A dog has the soul of a philosopher"* – Plato

When I was a young girl, I shared a sacred love with my dog, Ginger; a gentle Golden Retriever, who showed me the way through my childhood. Ginger came into my life when I was seven years old. I will never forget the day my mother told me and my siblings that we were going to see some Golden Retriever puppies and possibly adopt one to be our very own. Little did I know it at the time, but I was about to meet my new, best friend; a precious dog who would share my soul.

We all piled into the blue Rambler together and set off down the road. As we bounced along, my thoughts wandered… I didn't know exactly what a Golden Retriever was, but I did know that I loved dogs, any kind of dog. My first dog was a wolf-hybrid named Mukluk. I also had a Collie named Laddy, who was sweet and gentle. Secretly, I had always wished for a dog with floppy ears.

As we pulled into the driveway of an old, white farmhouse, I spotted the puppies playing in the yard. I was overjoyed to see that they had soft, golden fur and wonderful floppy ears, exactly like the kind of dog I had been wishing for! As soon as we entered the yard, all of the puppies instantly surrounded us, jumping up with uncontained excitement. Then, looking around, I noticed that there was one puppy in the yard that was a little more observant and contemplative. She was off by herself, watching us quietly. When we walked over to say hello, she eagerly got up to greet us; wiggling and waggling all the way. She kissed each one of us with her gentle, pink tongue and then snuggled sweetly into my lap. Soon she was fast asleep, peaceful and content. We all fell instantly in love with her and agreed that she was the special puppy we were looking for.

We waited patiently as my mother filled out the adoption papers. When everything was settled and the puppy was officially ours; I gathered her up in my arms and carried the adorable, little, golden ball of fluff to the car, to begin her new life with us.

On the way home, we talked about what we should name her. After some discussion, we decided to call her Ginger, for the gorgeous, golden color of her fur. I immediately spoke up to volunteer to be the person responsible for feeding and taking care of her. Everyone agreed and from that moment forward, Ginger had my full devotion. I spent all of my free time with her.

In almost every way, Ginger was a perfect dog. Like many Golden Retrievers, however, she had an excess amount of energy that needed to be channeled in a positive manner. She would tend to get overexcited when I came home from school and would knock me over when greeting me. Whenever I attempted to take her for a walk, she would pull me along on the leash, as I struggled to stay on my feet to keep up with her.

Finally, when I was nine years old, I asked my mom if I could join the local 4-H Club to learn about dog training. She agreed that it would be a good idea. From that time forward, once a week, Ginger and I attended dog training classes together. I was learning to be a dog handler, as Ginger was learning to be the best dog ever; easily mastering all of the obedience exercises. Soon we were participating in the local dog shows.

Ginger and I became a team. She was extremely smart and would do anything to please me. Every day after school, we would work together on perfecting all of the drills that she would be expected to perform. During those years, we received many awards, including a trophy at the Colorado State Fair. Ginger and I were two friends having fun and showing off what we could do together. We were constant companions who shared an unbreakable bond of love.

Childhood wasn't easy for me and I often felt lonely. Ginger was my comfort when I struggled with friendships and was bullied at school. I was shy and awkward and being with Ginger just allowed me to be who I was. She accepted me completely without judgment. She was my rock in a dysfunctional world. Whenever there were arguments in the family, I found my refuge with Ginger. I would curl up with her and tell her everything, and she always seemed to understand.

There was a lady living next door to me, who worked at the Denver Zoo. Sometimes, she would bring home animals in need of fostering and care. One day she brought home a baby jaguar that had been rejected by his mother and needed to be hand-raised. When I saw the little jaguar cub for the first time, I was absolutely enthralled. Although he was somewhat like a kitten, he had the look of the wild. His fur was buff-colored and he was covered from head to toe with black markings that looked like tiny paw prints. His ears pointed upwards like a kitten's ears, yet were rounded off at the tips. The feel of his fur through my fingers was soft and scruffy. He gazed at me curiously with pale turquoise eyes and I fell in love.

I learned that the jaguar's name was Tawny. In order to care for him properly, he was going to require frequent feedings and I offered to help. My neighbor showed me how to hold Tawny like a baby and give him his bottle. In my arms, the precious little jaguar cub would clutch the bottle sweetly between his paws, and suck eagerly. Afterward, he would fall asleep in my lap as I stroked his fur.

Every day after school, I would race home to help with the feedings. I loved caring for Tawny. Each day he was getting bigger and stronger. Finally, after three months, I was told that Tawny was strong enough to make it on his own at the zoo. It was time to let him go. I was devastated when I had to say goodbye, for we shared a special bond that I still remember to this day. My friendship with Tawny deepened my connection to the animal world.

Although many people question whether animals feel emotions or not, I am absolutely certain, beyond a doubt, that animals are emotional beings. To say that animals don't feel pain or have emotions is oftentimes used as an excuse to condone animal abuse. Animals suffer all around the world every day because of this notion. I know for certain that animals do feel pain and emotions. They experience love, fear, joy, jealousy, and grief. Animals sense and respond to what is in a person's heart. They are true and unwavering in their love and are not deceived by outer appearances. When an animal is in agony or pain, it may not be apparent at first because animals learn to hide their pain. In the wild, it is necessary for an animal to conceal any sign of weakness that will make them a vulnerable target for prey. Due to this behavior, people may not realize just how much an animal is suffering.

*He was only a fox like a hundred thousand other foxes.
But I have made him my friend, and now
he is unique in all the world."
– Antoine de Saint-Exupery, The Little Prince*

I've always felt that to earn the trust and friendship of any animal; either wild or domestic, is a great honor. One of the greatest honors I have ever received is the trust and friendship bestowed on me by a family of foxes. My friendship with this particular family of foxes has lasted for more than a decade, spanning many generations, and continues to this day.

It all began when my husband, Joe, and I moved to Sugarloaf Mountain west of Boulder, Colorado. When we first moved into our new home on the edge of the National Forest, we noticed two young foxes often playing together in the driveway. Upon observing their movements from the window, I soon came to realize that our new home also seemed to be their home. I discovered that they had a den nearby and they liked to frolic in our yard and snooze under the balcony. Our house had been vacant for many months before we moved in, so the foxes had made themselves at home. As far as they were concerned, Joe and I were the ones who had moved into their territory. We gave them respect and made a silent agreement that we would all co-exist together. They came to accept our presence and we accepted theirs. Over time, a deep friendship and trust grew between us.

In the beginning, we watched the foxes from a distance and they, in turn, watched us from afar with curiosity. One afternoon, as I knelt down to put some birdseed on the ground, I turned around and noticed that one of the little red foxes was standing right behind me, not more than four feet away. He stood there calmly, looking at me with trusting eyes; waiting patiently for me to put out more bird seed. At that moment, I understood that this little fox was the culprit who had been eating the birdseed at night. He looked at me with curiosity. He had no fear at all. As I gazed at him, his amber eyes penetrated my soul. He was reddish in color, with a white chest and gold and white markings on his face. On each leg, it looked like he was wearing a black sock. His coat was thick, fluffy, and very well groomed for a fox. I figured that he had been born in the spring and was probably about eight months old. He acted as if he already knew me and trusted me completely. I guess he had come to that conclusion after sensing my energy from a distance.

With stifled excitement, I stood there looking at him in wonder. For a long moment, neither one of us moved. Eventually, I decided to go inside the house to get my camera to photograph him. I backed away slowly and then rushed inside, hoping that he would still be there when I returned. To my surprise, he was still there, looking up at me from below the balcony. He stood calmly for me as I clicked away. I expected him to run, but he never did. He had no intention of going anywhere. He stayed and indicated to me that he wanted to be my friend. Joe and I decided to call him Foxy.

As Foxy grew more comfortable and accustomed to being around us, he often slept in the yard, all curled up in a ball, waiting for us to come outside. When I was gardening and doing other chores, Foxy would follow me around everywhere. Soon, he became more like a family dog than a fox and accompanied me to greet visitors. People didn't know what to think when they first saw me with Foxy by my side. It was a little awkward for me to try to explain why I had a fox following me around.

Out of the two foxes living on our property, Foxy was the brave one. He initiated the alliance first and we became fast friends. The other fox, who was Foxy's companion, was a little more bashful. I would see her skipping around in the woods at the outer periphery of our yard, watching us all, yet unsure if she should approach. Her energy was light and darting, like a fairy. She was fine and dainty, with very light-golden fur and white socks on each leg. Her amber colored eyes were mysterious and piercing. It was obvious to me that she was Foxy's girlfriend. We decided to call her Roxy.

In the early days of our friendship, Roxy was shy and cautious. She would come and play with Foxy when she didn't think I was looking. Sometimes she would wait under a certain tree for Foxy; all curled up in a ball, keeping one eye open with expectation, anticipating his return. Before long, Foxy would show up with a squirrel in his mouth for her. He would let Roxy take it and eat her fill, sharing a bite only after she was satisfied.

The following spring, Foxy and Roxy became proud parents. Roxy gave birth to four baby fox kits. Together they raised the precious babies that brought them such joy. Joe and I would often watch the fox kits wrestle and tumble, as they played in the yard. When they got old enough, Foxy would take them out to teach them how to hunt. The young foxes stayed around for several months and then gradually left, one by one, to find a mate and have families of their own.

For many years, in the springtime, a new litter of fox kits would emerge from under our shed. Every few years there would be a little black fox born in the litter. A black fox is actually the offspring of a red fox, displaying a recessive gene. Red foxes are born dark gray, and normally, their fur changes to gold and white as they mature. The black fox remains dark in color, except for a white tip at the end of its tail.

Early mornings and evenings, I would watch them all play in the meadow together. They were a close-knit family; loving, protecting, and caring for each other. The foxes stayed and lived happy, carefree lives on our property for many years. Sadly, however, one day a coyote discovered them and it became dangerous for them to stay in the area any longer. The foxes had to leave in order to save themselves.

After they left, three years passed before I saw any of the foxes again. During that time, I missed them terribly. Since then, one of Foxy and Roxy's daughters has returned. I call her, Mystic. She is the spitting image of Roxy, except for a dark star on her forehead. Being acutely aware of the coyote danger, Mystic would normally stay for only a day or so before moving on again. This past spring, however, she decided to come back to the place where she was born and raise her family in the forest behind our house. I pray for her safety and that her babies survive and thrive.

It is my belief that we are destined to connect with certain animals in our lives, just as we are destined in life to connect with certain people. I believe that an animal's soul is continuously evolving just as our own souls continue to evolve. Nurturing a relationship with an animal offers the animal an opportunity for growth, by what they may learn from us, just as we are offered an opportunity for growth, by what we might learn from them. Our animal brothers and sisters share the journey of life with us. We all originate from the same source. We are all connected.

Many people wonder whether animals have a language or not. In the animal world, there is a universal language of subtle body gestures and eye movements, as well as vocal inflections that they use to communicate with other animals. Even their breath holds clues to how they feel at any given moment. I've learned to notice these telling movements and to listen with all my senses in order to understand them. These communications are going on all the time. If you stop and listen to the birds, they are constantly communicating with each other. Their vocal sounds say a lot about how they are feeling. There are certain sounds for contentment and other sounds for anxiety or concern. I have learned to observe the subtle ways in which animals use their eyes, their posture, their voice, and their movements to express themselves. Animals also communicate using telepathic imagery; sending pictures from their minds that can be picked by other animals and humans. This is a natural process for them. As humans, we can pick up these telepathic images when we close our eyes and become meditative. This is the common ground where humans and animals can meet in order to connect and understand each other on a deeper level.

Many people have trouble understanding the language of animals. This is because people tend to see and interpret things from the limited perspective of a human being; rather than taking time to observe things from an animal's point of view. The language of animals is not something that can be taught but can only be learned by listening with the heart.

I have always been guided when an animal has come into my life. Today, my husband and I have three wonderful shelter dogs and two sweet kitties that we've rescued. Each beloved animal has a story about how they came to live with us. Every one of them has something to teach me. Somehow, they manage to point out my own inadequacies and help me to recognize how I can improve.

My mission is to speak for the animals that don't have a voice; to share the truth about them, and to let people know that they are intelligent and emotional beings. They love their families just as we love our families. It can be very painful emotionally for animals to be separated from one another when they share a deep bond. This is important to keep in mind when animals are bought, sold, traded, and adopted. They are at our mercy and we must try our best to make good decisions for them, and always take into account, their physical and emotional well-being.

All over the planet, animals are abused, tortured, and discarded in the name of making a profit. It's imperative for each one of us to sort out our feelings about what is right and wrong; to contemplate within our hearts where we stand on the humane treatment of animals. As consciousness spreads, one by one, people will begin to change their attitudes. It is vital that we teach the children and the generations coming after us, that animals must be respected and protected.

The more time I spend with animals, the more I see into their souls and understand how much like us they are. They need guardians to speak for them and to protect them as they struggle for survival on this planet, for this world is their world too.

*"Each moment contains a hundred messages from God."*
*-Rumi*

# Chapter 9

## Whisperings from the Universe

I believe that no matter where we go in life, we are accompanied by a Holy Presence that guides and protects us. In every moment, there is a voice that whispers within and there are signs and symbols to help us find our way. Messages from Spirit come in a myriad of ways. A message may come in the form of a bird, a butterfly, a rainbow, or a child's smile. An answer, to a burning question, may be revealed in a random conversation that one hears in passing, or in the lyrics of a song on the radio.

When we become quiet, tune in, and allow Spirit to speak, we are able to receive these messages. It depends on where we place our attention that will determine whether or not we notice, or fully grasp, the significance of the messages that are being presented to us. Keep in mind that every living thing, every person, and every creature on this planet is a manifestation and an extension of the One. When we honor our intimate connections to the Originating Life Force, to each other, and to all living things; we open ourselves to the infinite web of consciousness, sometimes referred to as The Mind of God. It is through this web that we are all connected.

In truth, the Creative Force of God is flowing through you and pulsating throughout your being at all times. You are a part of everything that exists. God is within you, just as you are within God. When you truly understand, from the depths of your soul, that you are never separate from God, but rather, that you are an extension of God; your personal power increases exponentially. When you come to trust that you are forever surrounded in love, then you know with certainty that in every moment, you are walking with Spirit.

When you realize that no matter how things appear, there is always a larger force at play in the universal scheme of life; you gain an elevated perspective and an understanding that nothing is ordinary, and nothing is mundane. Life is teeming with mysteries, serendipities, and profound coincidences. It is when you take time to practice stillness, with an open mind and heart that you will be most receptive to the communications from the higher realms. For instance, you may receive "letters from heaven" from loved ones who have passed. They may send a feather, a bird, an insect, or an animal; or they may shape a cloud into an image that holds meaning for you. It all boils down to whether you choose to pay attention and embrace the messages, or simply dismiss them. Here is an example of how a message from another realm might manifest.

Last year, my dear friend John, left this world. A few days after his passing, I was outside playing in the yard with my two dogs, Déjà and Starla. Suddenly, Déjà became distracted by something on the other side of the yard. As I watched from a distance, I could see her sniffing something up close on the ground and then playfully jumping back while waving her paws in the air. I couldn't imagine what was causing her to behave in such a peculiar way. If it were a small squirrel or bunny, she would be chasing it around; but instead, she pawed at whatever it was, tenderly and good-naturedly.

I walked over to see what Déjà was up to. To my utter amazement, I saw that she was playing with an enormous, black, Scarab Beetle! It was about the size of my hand. I asked Déjà to back away and looked down on it with wonder. The Scarab Beetle stood there with quite a presence, waving its antennae wildly in the air. In all my years of living in Colorado, I had never seen anything like it. It was extremely unusual and absolutely stunning. At that moment, I remembered that before John left this world, he had promised to send me a sign when he made it to the other side. I knew instantly that this Scarab Beetle held a message for me from my beloved friend. The sacred Scarab Beetle is an Egyptian symbol for Khepri, the Sun God associated with resurrection. John was sending me a message; reassuring me that death is an illusion and indeed he lives on, in eternity. Knowing this, gave me great consolation.

The next morning, after this incident occurred, I found nine, pure white feathers, lying on the blue welcome mat outside my door. I don't know how these magnificent, white feathers managed to appear in a perfect cluster on my welcome mat, but there they were. Each feather was seven to nine inches long and there are no birds in the area that I could identify, with feathers like that. Many folks believe that a white feather is considered to be an angel feather; sent to let you know that your loved one on the other side is safe and well. A white feather is also a sign of faith and protection. Feathers represent a connection to the spiritual realms and to divinity. They are a symbol of flight and freedom, not just physically, but also in a spiritual sense.

Delving deeper into the mystical meaning of the message that was left for me on the modest welcome mat outside my door; I recognized the significance of the fact that there were exactly nine feathers. The number nine is used to define the perfect movement of God and is a symbol for Divine completeness. John was letting me know that he was safe and free on the other side of the veil and that all was perfect and complete.

This is how ethereal communication works; through pictures, metaphors and symbols. When you take time to notice what is going on around you, you will discover that the Universe has important messages for you and there are many ways in which these communications might be delivered. For instance; it is important to pay attention when you find yourself having recurring experiences. Most likely, the Universe is asking you to become aware of something. If you begin to see repeating numbers on license plates, addresses, birth dates, or phone numbers throughout your day, take notice. Numbers carry the frequency of the Universe and these numbers may very well hold hidden meanings that you may want to investigate. If you find random animals or insects showing up in indiscriminate places, this may also be a message from the Universe.

Have you ever had the experience, when going about your day, that you repeatedly see someone who bears an uncanny resemblance to a long, lost friend? When this happens, it can be a nudge from the Universe, telling you that it's time to call your friend. There are many types of random occurrences that might indicate that you are being guided by a higher power. For instance, if you find yourself having a chance meeting with someone who is the perfect person who can help you in a matter that you are pursuing; this is confirmation from the Universe that you are on the right path. Another way you may receive a message is through a gut-feeling or emotion. If you have an unsettled feeling about something, such as a sudden unexplained fear of impending danger; listen to those feelings and use caution.

The Universe communicates through symbols, metaphors, coincidences, and random occurrences. It has been during the times when I have faced my greatest challenges that I have found guidance in the quiet voice of Spirit. I have discovered that the secret to living a life that is in alignment with my soul's highest purpose; is to open my heart , trust, pay attention, and tune into the whisperings of the Universe for guidance.

Whatever is happening in any one moment is perfectly timed and executed. It is when you try to control everything, down to the last precise detail, that things don't flow well. When you approach life with an agenda and disregard the wisdom of the voice within; when you try to "push the river", you get out of sync with the flow of the Universe. Trust that there is a reason for everything that occurs. If you miss a deadline, or things happen that are beyond your control, just relax and let go. It could be that you are being protected by an unforeseen delay, orchestrated by a higher power to keep you out of harm's way.

Every now and then, the "Angels of Change" will swoop into your life to hand you a new interest or lead you towards a new path. When you feel a strong urge to make a change in your life; whether it is to move to a new place or to begin a new career, listen to that voice inside you and honor your quest. Your dreams are worth pursuing. Trust the guidance that is being offered and recognize that there is a higher power working through every person you encounter. The right people will be put in your path to help lead you towards your destiny.

You can also receive spiritual communications through dreams. Before going to sleep at night, you may want to set an intention to receive guidance or find a solution to a problem that you have been struggling with. Oftentimes, in the morning you will simply know what you need to do next, in order to solve your problem. Even if you don't consciously remember the dream, you will wake up with clarity about what steps you need to take. You will be able to see your path clearly, open and unobstructed before you.

Divine guidance is delivered through serendipitous events that happen in your life. Nothing should ever be brushed off as mere coincidence. People will be placed in your path for a reason. Perhaps, making their acquaintance will be significant in leading you one more step toward your destiny. It is also possible that a person will be placed in your path because you are destined to play a significant role in that individual's life.

When you hold the presence of God in your heart, everybody you come into contact with, will be touched and blessed. When you offer yourself as a channel for Divine love, you will be guided to the ones who need you most. As a soul inhabiting a physical body on this planet, it is always important to remember that your true home is with Spirit. Your job is to stay plugged into the infinite Life Force and radiate your light out into the world. Strive to recognize the sacred divinity each moment holds.

# Part Two
## Spiritual Alchemy

*"The wound is the place where light enters you."*
*- Rumi*

# Chapter 10
## Dissolving the Dream of What is Not True

The secret to becoming authentically free, and creating the life you truly desire, is to be willing to uncover, examine, and take a good hard look at the core wounds and false beliefs that are hiding in the recesses of your heart and mind. A core wound is the deepest, most profound source of emotional pain that hides within you. It affects the way you look at life and how you feel about yourself. If you harbor a core wound that is left unaddressed; it will continue to fester, limiting your ability to experience true freedom, joy, and authenticity in your life, and your relationships.

Everything that has ever happened to you, during infancy and childhood, has played a very significant role in shaping your belief system about your value as a person. Whether you experienced rejection, abandonment, fear, or any other kind of trauma that cut deep into your psyche; those residual core wounds continue to influence your feelings of self-worth and how you relate to others.

If core wounds are not addressed, they can morph into a toxic stew of deep-seated anger, sadness, and depression. These wounds must be exposed in order to heal consciously and separate lies from the truth. Failure to deal with these wounds can lead to engaging in avoidance behaviors such as alcoholism, drug addiction, working excessively, watching too much TV, or disassociating from the world in other ways. Core wounds also have an effect on physical health and can be a source of chronic stress and fatigue. Unprocessed traumas and emotions take up residence inside the tissues of the body. This can be very detrimental and ultimately manifest in the form of some kind of physical ailment or disease.

Most of us, at some point early on in our lives, suffered from some kind of emotional or physical trauma; brought on by a particular event or situation that left us feeling confused, hurt and shattered. As children, we may have experienced disapproval or punishment from parents, elders or peers; simply for being our authentic selves. From the perspective of a child; at the time of these occurrences, it was impossible to process the feelings and emotions that surrounded an event, accurately. As a result, we oftentimes interpreted things falsely; blaming ourselves and concluding that on some deep level there was something inherently wrong with us. We internalized the shame we felt. Even today, we may continue to blame ourselves for things that were never our fault. In an attempt to shield our hearts; the residual emotional pain that we still carry from past events may cause us to put up protective, psychological barriers and become isolated.

The hidden pain of a core wound can weigh you down and cloud the expression of your being. For this reason, it is essential to be willing to uncover the wounds of the past and bring everything into the light. As an adult, it will be easier to look back upon painful events from the viewpoint of a detached onlooker. This will empower you to perceive the situation with more clarity; rather than viewing the experience through the eyes of a scared, helpless child. You will be able to understand how you may have misinterpreted an event and why you may still be blaming yourself for something you never did. Facing your past can be scary, but it is only in acknowledging your pain, and looking at it from a non-threatening perspective, that you will be able to process your emotions and heal from the hurt and the shame that still haunts you.

As young, innocent children, we looked to others for validation and began to believe what we were being told about ourselves. We developed a set of core beliefs that defined how we viewed ourselves and the world. We learned how to love others by the way in which we were loved. We learned to receive and accept love according to how it was given to us. As children, we attempted to find acceptance in society by inventing ourselves based on the perceptions and expectations of others.

The core beliefs that we formed as children are called "schemas". These schemas are adopted and integrated into our own personal belief systems and become a part of who we are. Once this happens, it is very difficult to separate fact from fiction or to identify and overcome false beliefs. By the time a child reaches twelve years of age, these beliefs are firmly set into place. The schemas that we adopt as children play an enormous role in how we feel about ourselves, and how we view the world. Much of the dark, dense energy that we carry inside us, is not our own. We have picked it up from others; including parents, teachers, siblings, friends, and peers. All of the experiences and interactions that we have had with other people have wielded great influence in the development of the core beliefs that we formed as children.

There are many different types of schemas. These set patterns of thinking seep into a person's consciousness and can impair and prevent them from attaining the full expression of who they are meant to be. These beliefs can manifest in many ways. For instance, a particular distorted belief can morph into a fear that can eventually take over a person's life. It might manifest as a fear of an impending disaster; where a person feels that something beyond their control could strike at any time, or it could be a fear of a looming crisis such as financial loss, serious illness, or deep emotional loss. These types of fears can keep a person stuck; causing them to feel paralyzed and afraid to move forward in life. There are numerous fears that may affect an individual. For example; one might have a fear of not being liked or a fear of not being able to handle day-to-day responsibilities. Other fears may include a fear of expressing one's own opinions, a fear of abandonment, a fear of not being adequate, or a fear of failure. These fears prevent a person from fulfilling their dreams and destiny.

When children suffer from emotional and physical abuse, they learn not to trust others. As a result, in an effort to hide from the world, they may begin to live in a protective shell. Overcoming a deep distrust of others is one of the most difficult of all the schemas to conquer. In particular, children who are raised by alcoholic parents are oftentimes deeply traumatized and live their lives with a sense of shame and embarrassment. Not only have they suffered from the scorn and rejection directed towards their family due to their parents' alcoholism, but children of alcoholics also suffer the horrors of living in an insane and unpredictable environment, where their parents may become angry or violent.

Children, who are shattered by trauma, don't have the skills to understand or manage their pain. They may not even be able to approach their caretakers for help because oftentimes, it's their caretakers who are causing their pain. As these wounded children go through life, they may experience anxiety, and depression, as well as feelings of guilt, shame, and anger. Feeling empty, alone, and unlovable, they may also experience relationship problems and have trouble trusting or bonding with others.

In order to cope, children will oftentimes turn to something outside of themselves to fill the void and survive. Due to the fact that they are unable to deal with their feelings, wounded children will do their best to numb out in some way. Initially, they may isolate themselves or turn to food, TV, or video games in order to find comfort and consolation. Later on, as children grow older, they may use drugs or alcohol to cover their feelings of inadequacy and to mask their insecurities. This is how addictions begin.

Take a moment now to reflect on what your core beliefs are. Try to identify how these beliefs got started and how they are holding you back, keeping you stuck. Was there a traumatic childhood event that triggered the onslaught of a fear or phobia that you still carry today? Beginning from the moment of your birth, reflect on how you were received and welcomed into the world by those who cared for you. Were you a cherished child or were you an unwanted child? All of these factors played a significant role in the development of your belief system that dictates how you experience the world.

What is your overall feeling about your own self-worth? Do you feel like you are worthy of love? Do you have a sense of belonging, or do you feel like you are flawed and will never be good enough? Do you feel as if you need to apologize for even being here on this planet? Do you allow yourself to slip into the background and withhold your soul's mission, for fear of being criticized? When you can consciously identify your schemas, you can begin to unravel the distorted beliefs about yourself that have held you captive and prevented you from expressing your true essence.

All of these fears and core beliefs must be identified and eradicated from your consciousness. When you take the time to think back on your childhood and identify how the beliefs you formed as a child are still affecting you today; only then, will you be able to move forward and free yourself from repetitive behavioral patterns. When you are able to recognize a particular schema, write it down and ask yourself, "Where is the evidence to support this belief?" As an adult, you will be able to interpret these events differently and see them for what they are. You will be able to see the whole picture from a less threatening point of view. As you view things with more clarity, you can begin to sort out the truth from misconceptions. Sorting through your core beliefs will give you the power to change your narrative about who you truly are.

Core beliefs also play a role and have a pervasive influence over one's relationships. These beliefs dictate the ways in which a person adapts and finds acceptance among others; the ways in which one interacts with the world in order to get their needs met. A child learns through modeling another person's behavior. For example, aggression in children can be traced to an aggressive role model.

Try to identify if there has been somebody in your own life who influenced you to the degree that you chose to model their behavior. Exploring the schemas that you have adopted throughout your lifetime, will reveal much about the core wounds you carry. It is important to remember that you are not the wounded part of yourself. Your beautiful essence is the spark of God that dwells within you. In order to retrieve your inner child and reclaim your divine nature, you need to be willing to honor your feelings and bring up the pain that you have buried inside.

You may think of your feelings as an inner guidance system. They are the voice of your soul in your body. As you allow your feelings to come to the surface, listen carefully and be willing to be there for your lost, wounded child. In order to let go of the pain that you carry within you, it will help to begin a conversation with your higher self. Ask for clarity and truth as you set out to explore and uncover the false beliefs that have been holding you back and hindering your soul's expression. Ask what you need to do in order to heal your inner child. Allow the information and impressions to pop into your mind. Once you understand the steps you need to follow, make a commitment to take loving action to heal your deepest, emotional wounds. As you do this, the heaviness in your soul will lift, and you will begin to feel lighter, less anxious, and less depressed. Focus on your heart and make a decision to treat yourself lovingly. Your inner child will eventually feel safe enough to come out of hiding, and you will begin to reconnect with the parts of you that have been abandoned along the way.

Once you feel as though you have successfully been able to recover and integrate the missing parts of yourself, it is time to take another look at your life. With a new belief system in place, look at the world around you with new eyes and an open heart. What is being reflected back to you? Everything that appears before you now, is the result of all of your previous thoughts and perceptions that have brought you to the present moment. Take note of everything. What is your environment reflecting? What is your body telling you? Keep in mind, everything is written in metaphors. The material manifestation of your reality is an energetic replica of your belief system. As you change your beliefs, everything in your world will also change.

Imagination is the tool that we have been given in order to communicate and co-create with the Universe. When we consciously use the intensity of our thoughts, together with passion, desire, and clear imagination; the secret to consciously creating our lives unfolds. The language of the Universe is written in the pictures we send forth from our minds. When we learn to use our imaginations to consciously form and send out mental pictures; we can manifest anything we desire and communicate telepathically with all living beings. As we become aware of the images we are sending out and how they are being reflected back to us, we learn to harness the power of the Universal Mind of God. It is important to remember that the Universe will give us exactly what we ask for and expect. It listens and responds to every thought precisely. Whatever we focus our attention on, dictates exactly what we will attract into our lives. For this reason, it is vital that we become aware of our thoughts, our self-talk, and above all, not to focus on fear.

Sometimes, we may succumb to the temptation to blame others for any unfortunate situation that we find ourselves in. It is important to remember that we are the ones who are the architects of our lives. Keep in mind that some difficulties that present themselves may be the result of past karma that must be worked through and resolved.

If you were to observe your life as an objective witness and relay your story right now, what would your story be? Would you portray yourself as a victim? Would there be an abundance of resources or would there be scarcity in your life? Would somebody else be to blame for your hardships? If you do not like the story you are participating in, you must change your narrative in order to change your reality.

Life is but a dream, and you have the power to wake up at any moment to change it at any time. Examine the dream you are currently engaged in and the roles in life that you play. These roles are not necessarily reflective of who you truly are. These roles may falsely define you. Oftentimes, in order to satisfy certain expectations from others, it's possible that you may choose to adopt a role or display a certain personification that doesn't portray your authentic self. It is more like you are playing a character in a dream. Each role that you play is accompanied by certain social requirements. Some of these roles are defined by the interpersonal relationships that you were born into, such as the relationships you share with family members.

Oftentimes, people will take on a particular role in order to help them cope with challenging circumstances. They may try to hide their vulnerabilities behind the roles that they play. For example, in order to exert a sense of control over one's life, a person may assume a role in the guise of a powerful figure such as a judge, an authoritarian, or a strict disciplinarian. If one feels weak, lacks confidence, or is unwilling to participate in life; that person may take on the role of being a helpless, passive victim, in order to gain sympathy or to avoid taking responsibility. A person may also adopt a particular role in order to mask the ego's agenda.

Until we uncover our true essence, we live life like actors on a stage; presenting a personification that we have adapted over time. As we become more conscious, we can begin to sort out and navigate the labyrinth that will lead us back to the truth of who we really are.

Wake up from the dream of what is not true and rediscover your soul's purpose. Choose to live the life you were meant to live. Stay forever connected to the Great Mind of God; for it is in this realm that you can transcend the dream and gain access to the infinite power of the Universe.

*"A little while, a moment of rest upon the wind,
and another woman shall bear me."*
*- Kahlil Gibran*

# Chapter 11
## Winds of Karma

Our lives unfold as a mystery, unwinding in time. At some point, we all contemplate the questions: *Why are we here? What is our purpose? Is there a deeper meaning to life, and to our relationships? Why are some people born into poverty while others are born into a life of privilege?* Sometimes, life just doesn't seem fair.

Have you ever had the feeling that you have lived before? Have you ever visited a new place that felt strangely familiar? Have you ever met somebody and felt an instant recognition? One explanation for these feelings can be found in the concept of reincarnation; in which a soul is born into a physical body, dies, and returns to spirit form, only to be born again into a new body. If you accept the notion that we are spiritual beings having a physical experience; then it stands to reason that the spiritual journey not only encompasses the evolution of the soul in one lifetime but also involves many lifetimes.

Reincarnation is a process of refining and liberating the soul. The belief in reincarnation is widespread. References can be found in ancient Egypt, as well as in Eastern religions such as Hinduism and Buddhism. In the Western world, past life regressions are commonly conducted and investigated. There are many documented stories and incidences that lend validation to the concept of reincarnation.

After having had several out-of-body experiences myself, where I retained conscious awareness outside of my physical form; the idea of reincarnation seems very plausible to me. I know that my soul is free and is not limited to my body.

As humans, our identities and personalities are constantly changing, however, within the soul, there is an everlasting essence that exists as pure awareness. The soul serves as a witness and observer of our lives, independent of our physicality. This awareness is known as soul consciousness. As evolving souls, we are on a timeless, eternal journey. Every lifetime is another step towards gaining wisdom and enlightenment.

It is my belief that there are no coincidences or random occurrences. Rather, there is a deep, profound purpose and an underlying meaning for everything that happens. I have witnessed too many miracles and serendipitous events to dismiss the evidence that there is indeed an unseen force that guides the course of our lives. In my pursuit to understand the spiritual implications of the intricacies of the Universe; I have been led to trust that for each soul entity, there is a predestined path that will ultimately lead to one's destiny; however, each individual has their own free-will and the power to choose how their life will unfold.

When we come to this planet, we come with a personal mission to fulfill. Each one of us carries the seeds of wisdom, along with the skills and talents that we have mastered and acquired over many lifetimes. There is a plan in place for our lives, and along the way, there are lessons to be learned. Even before we were born, each one of us made a spiritual contract with our higher self. We agreed to take on a new life and to work through accumulated karma, be it positive or negative, in order to evolve on a soul level.

Relationships with significant others have already been predetermined. There are souls we are destined to meet again, with whom we have shared a bond of love over countless lifetimes; and there are souls with whom we have had previous difficulties and there is past karma to be resolved. These reunions are predestined. Those souls we have known before will inevitably show up in our lives to play significant roles. It follows a Universal Law that any unsettled karma that we share with another person, must be confronted and worked through to completion.

Before a soul incarnates on Earth, it is said that a decision is made, with the help of Spirit Guides, to determine what the incoming soul's life purpose will be. An ideal family is then selected that will provide the perfect learning environment, best suited for that particular soul's unfolding. On the level of soul consciousness, each person has agreed to the arrangement that will be most optimal for their spiritual growth. This may include great challenges and hardships that one must overcome.

The relationships we share with others are the forces that help to sculpt our lives. The dynamics of a relationship bring up circumstances that teach us about who we are. In relationships, various situations arise at the most appropriate times to challenge our souls. We have all experienced hurt, pain, anger, and emotional upheaval in our interactions with others. Whenever two or more people come together, it is inevitable that there are significant lessons to be learned. Ultimately, relationships test us in every way and instruct us in the path of the heart.

When we go through difficult experiences, it leaves a profound impact on our psyches and helps us to get clarity about what we don't want in our lives. This leads us to forsake everything that doesn't serve our higher purpose and urges us to move forward to consciously create a better future. As we work to balance the karmic dues that we share with others, eventually there will be healing and resolution. As we free ourselves from past karmic ties, we will begin to attract new people into our lives whose vibrations synchronize with our own highest aspirations.

Keep in mind that the souls and circumstances in your life are the powers that guide your journey. Remember that the characters, who are present in your life today, may be the same souls with whom you have shared many, many incarnations. It is possible that you have encountered each other before in numerous different roles; such as lovers, parents, teachers, children, friends, or enemies. Whatever the previous relationship with another person has been, it is destiny that brings you back together again. The exact moment in time is prearranged. This means that in an instant, you can be walking down the street and suddenly collide into somebody with whom you are destined to share life's journey. When this happens, there is an electrifying spark that re-ignites, and from that point forward, life takes a new turn.

I'm sure that you have had the experience of meeting a person and feeling as though you have always known them. Instantly, there is a natural and easy connection. When you meet someone with whom you are destined to share your life, it will feel much different than other passing introductions and acquaintances. It is said that when two souls come together who have known each other before; a phenomenon occurs that is known as "soul recognition". On a deep internal level, a memory stirs between the two souls. It may not be on a conscious level, but there will be an inner knowing; a feeling that tugs at the heart, that draws these people irresistibly together.

When this happens to you, you may feel extremely intrigued or attracted to a certain person, or you may even have dreams about them, before you actually meet on the physical plane. Even if the shared karma from a past lifetime isn't of a positive nature, you will still feel drawn to a person because of soul recognition. The reunion is preordained and past karma must be reconciled. There may be a feeling of ecstasy when you first meet, such as in "love at first sight", or you may be brought together by circumstance for just a short time, in order to work through a karmic obligation. If you have unfinished business with another soul, nothing will keep you apart until your shared karma is resolved.

This phenomenon also occurs with groups of souls who incarnate together for a common purpose. Any type of group can serve to attract and bring souls together who have unfinished karma to work through or a shared destiny to fulfill. Group karma can involve nations, towns, schools, bands, political parties, co-workers, or any group of people.

In addition to group karma, all souls living on Earth during any particular time period, also share global karma. This is evident today as our planet, and all of the sentient beings living on it, are facing dire consequences due to the environmental policies that are being implemented around the world at this time. These policies will ultimately have an impact on us all, as well as future generations. We are all participants in creating and resolving global karma. Therefore, it is important to remember that in addition to being a citizen of a community or nation, each one of us has a responsibility to take care of our world as a global citizen of planet Earth.

As we become more aware of the dynamics of our various relationships, we begin to appreciate and recognize that the mere fact we are sharing a physical existence with a particular soul at a particular time, is a miracle. Love endures throughout eternity. The force of love connects us and draws us back to those we have known and loved before. Love is never lost and does not die when the body dies. Love transcends all. Each relationship that we have with another person is a promise fulfilled in an agreement that was made in another space and time.

As you sail through the karmic winds of your own destiny, keep your heart and mind open. It is possible that in an instant, you may encounter a cherished soul whom you have been waiting for lifetimes to meet again, and the miraculous moment has finally arrived!

*"If you wish to understand the Universe, think of energy, frequency and vibration."* —*Nikola Tesla*

# Chapter 12
## Your Energetic Signature

Energy is all there is. It is the life force that sustains us all. Even though the physical world seems to be solid; in truth, we exist in an infinite sea of moving energy that is malleable. The energetic Universe begins with the atom. In each atom, there is an originating pulse of vibration. Quantum Physics tells us that the atom is actually an invisible force field, composed of negatively charged electrons whirling around a positively charged nucleus. The atom is a kind of miniature tornado that emits waves of electrical energy.

Our bodies are a collection of atoms and energy systems. Each cell is like a tiny battery that carries 1.4 volts of electricity. This may not seem like much, however, when multiplied by fifty trillion, which is the approximate number of cells in the human body, it adds up to a strong electromagnetic energy field. This energy, sometimes referred to as Chi, Qui or Prana, can be transferred to another person through hands-on-healing.

Each atom has its own frequency or vibration. When two atomic waves of energy connect, they are either in synch with each other, which creates a harmonious effect, or they are out of synch, resulting in a destructive, annulling effect. As human beings, we are both transmitters and receivers of energy. Energy is contagious. We are all touched and influenced by the energy around us.

Every individual has their own energetic signature. This is a vibration that is unique and cannot be disguised. A person's energetic signature reveals more about them than the words that they speak. It reflects their past, their beliefs, their dominant thoughts, and their outlook on life. All living things respond to energetic frequencies.

The emotions that we feel and the thoughts that we think are sent out into the ethers as energy in motion. Each one of us is responsible for the effect that we have on other people and the physical environment around us. If our vibrations are filled with love and harmony, the surrounding environment will reflect that back to us. The Universal Sea of Energy, which infuses and vitalizes everything around us, is dynamic and constantly changing. We are all active participants in this great cosmic dance.

It is important to become mindful of how your own energy is affecting others. It is also imperative to become aware of the energy around you and how it is influencing your well-being. If you feel negative energy coming at you from another person, it is not necessary for you to blindly consent to be a recipient of that energy. You are in control. If somebody is angry, or impatient, or acting in a condescending manner towards you, do not take on their energy as your own. It's easy to get entangled in an energetic exchange with someone, where blame and negativity get passed back and forth like a hot potato. Instead of becoming caught up in this kind of a trap; you can alter the encounter by consciously elevating your own energy to focus on love and forgiveness. This will change the energetic frequency of the situation and lead to a better outcome. By deliberately raising your own vibration, you have the power to be an uplifting and inspiring example for others, helping to create a better world.

Energy has intelligence and memory. Every thought that we think and every emotion that we experience leaves a lingering imprint. Our energetic vibrations have an effect on everything we touch and interact with. This is why certain places invoke a particular feeling. The atmosphere vibrates with history from the past. Whenever anything happens, there is a residual artifact of energy left behind that is tangible and can be felt. This is the basic premise for psychometry; a form of extrasensory perception in which a person can sense or read the history of an object by merely touching it. Everything has an energetic emission and leaves an impression behind.

The less visible something is to the naked eye, the higher its vibration. Thoughts, emotions, and consciousness all vibrate at a high frequency. Words are invisible thoughts that are shared by means of invisible sound waves. When speaking, the words that we use have a tremendous influence on those around us. It is through the frequencies of sound that we can align ourselves with the power of the Universe. Sound acts as a universal language that connects all beings. Whether we are using words or music, we communicate by means of vibration.

Your personal frequency goes out like a radio wave in all directions from the center of your being. Frequency attracts frequency. Those who vibrate at a similar frequency to your own will be able to tune in and receive your energetic signals. The magnetism that you exude determines the kind of energy you attract into your life. Be clear about what kind of people you want to spend your time with and they will be magically drawn to you. If you send out good vibrations, the Universe will respond by mirroring back that energy in return. This is known as "The Law of Attraction".

Each one of us has a choice, rooted in free will, about whether we want to take the path of positivity or negativity. In any moment we can choose to turn a negative situation into a positive one; simply by making an empowering decision about what kind of energy we want in our lives. Remember, it is up to each one of us to take steps to protect our own happiness and to guard against negativity. In every encounter and situation, it is our responsibility to set the tone.

One of the best ways to help steer a negative person towards positivity is to set an example by personally expressing an enthusiastic outlook on life. We can uplift others by showing them that we care about them. If a person seems to be perpetually sad or has a dismal point of view in general, this is an indication that they need somebody to shine a light into their darkness; to give them a sense of joy and hope. People who are struggling with negativity need love, compassion, and understanding.

Strive for happiness. Socrates once said, "Happiness flows not from physical or external conditions, such as bodily pleasures or wealth and power, but from living a life that's right for your soul, your deepest good."

When you make a conscious choice to be happy, you exude the vibration of happiness and become like a magnet; attracting joyful people and positive situations into your life. In order to cultivate true happiness for yourself, it is important to focus on your heart and all that you are grateful for. Acknowledge and appreciate all of the blessings in your life. Make every effort to be positive and to look for the best in people. Develop empathy and patience, and take time to be kind to yourself and to others. Do your best to let go of stress and live in the moment. Pay attention to your self-talk. Make sure that you are giving yourself encouraging and inspiring messages. When you make a decision to live a positive life and take conscious steps towards being happy, you can trust that the Universe will support you in your endeavors.

Never underestimate the power of your presence in any situation. When you stand strong and confident in love, peace, and harmony, everybody around you will be touched. You can hold space for others without uttering a word. At the core of your being, you vibrate as perfection. Focus on your inner light and you will radiate the attributes of divinity.

*"The world of reality has its limits;
the world of imagination is boundless."*
–Jean-Jacques Rousseau

# Chapter 13
## Understanding Brain Wave Frequencies

Initially, the notion that we are responsible for creating our own reality seems to be a vague concept. In order to unleash our full, unlimited, God-given potential, it is necessary to gain an understanding of brain wave frequencies and how to use them consciously and effectively. We all possess this latent power within us. We can tap into it at any time for self-improvement, to better our lives and the lives of others.

Most of us use only a very small portion of our brains. In order to use the full power of our minds to create our lives with intention, it is necessary to learn about the different states of mind that are available to us and how to access them. This is a key component in manifesting reality.

Our brains pulsate at different wave frequencies. In 1929, German physiologist, Hans Berger, discovered that the brain emits faint electrical impulses that are identified with different states of consciousness. The brain emits vibration and the rate of vibration is measured in cycles per second. This is what is known as brain wave frequency. When we are functioning in our normal, everyday waking state, this active state of mind is referred to as the beta frequency.

In 1944, scientific researcher, Dr. Jose Silva, discovered that human intelligence can also learn to function with awareness at slower brain wave frequencies, known as the alpha and theta brain states. This was a very significant discovery. It enabled people to learn how to consciously slow down their brain waves in order to gain access to a greater portion of their brain power. Speaking to deeper levels of the mind is a little like self-hypnosis. It enables a person to gain control and assume a position of mastery over their mind.

It's essential to understand that the mind will believe everything it is told. Our brains are very similar to computers. They operate electrically and are capable of storing and retrieving information. The brain and the computer are both problem solvers and respond accordingly to the programming they receive. For this reason, it is vital that you become aware of your own self-talk and the thoughts and energies that you allow to enter your consciousness. You must be the guardian at the gate of your mind, and the ruler of the kingdom within. If you don't take control of your mind, somebody else will, and you will find yourself in a constant reactive state to the energy around you. When you fail to take control of your mind, you permit the influence of others to dictate your experience. You absorb their energy and their programming as your own.

## There are Five Principal Brain Waves Frequencies

**The Gamma Brain Wave Frequency** is the most recently discovered type of brain wave. It is the highest brain wave frequency, cycling between forty and one hundred cycles per second. It's been found that when a person meditates regularly, the brain produces more gamma waves. This state helps to reduce stress, anxiety, and depression and is associated with feeling blessed and grateful. People who are functioning in the gamma state, exhibit more empathy and compassion toward others. Gamma brain waves are associated with peak concentration and extremely high levels of cognitive functioning.

**The Beta Brain Wave Frequency** is associated with a person's outer conscious levels. This includes engaging in day-to-day activities, taking in the world through the five senses, and interacting in social situations with others. In the beta state, the brain pulsates between fourteen to forty cycles per second. When a person is in their normal, active waking state, they are functioning in beta.

**The Alpha Brain Wave Frequency** is linked to a state of deep physical and mental relaxation. When one learns to slow down their brain wave frequency to access the alpha state of mind; it is possible to engage the powers of creativity, imagination, and intuition in order to influence reality. In the alpha state of mind, the brain wave frequency cycles between seven and fourteen pulsations per second. This brain wave frequency is about half that of the normal waking state. The alpha state of mind is associated with inner levels of mental activity such as tranquility, inspiration, accelerated healing, clairvoyance, daydreaming, and hypnosis. Young children normally function in the alpha state up to the age of seven years old. Animals also function in the alpha state. By slowing down the brain waves to the alpha state of mind, it is possible to communicate with children and animals on a deep, intuitive level. From the alpha state of mind, one can use the power of imagination to create the world of their dreams.

**The Theta Brain Wave Frequency** is related to greater learning and recall capabilities. The brain wave frequency for the theta state is between four to seven pulsations per second. The theta brain wave governs the part of the mind that lies between the conscious and the unconscious and retains memories and feelings. Theta is the state we are functioning in when we enter the first phase of a dream.

**The Delta Brain Wave** is associated with deep sleep and periods of unconsciousness. In this state, the brain wave frequency pulsates between one-half to four pulsations per second.

## How to Use Your Mind to Unlock Your Inner Genius

In order to gain control of your mind and release its full potential; it is of utmost importance to become aware of the full range of brain wave frequencies, and to learn how to use them to your advantage.

During sleep, the brain activity moves through the alpha, theta, and delta states; just as a tide moves through the ocean. In order to achieve success in your manifestation work, you will want to focus on functioning in the alpha state of consciousness. This is where positive thinking exerts its power. It is where prayers are answered. In the alpha state, you can tap into the resources of Universal Energy and Intelligence, as you set out to create the reality you desire.

When you are at the edge of sleep and waking, you are in the alpha state. Most people are functioning in the alpha state during the last thirty minutes of sleep. This is a good place to begin when you are first learning to access the alpha state to program your mind and engage in conscious manifestation work. As you awaken from sleep, slowly and mindfully, you will gain an understanding of what it feels like to be in the alpha state.

You can practice reaching the alpha state of mind by simply closing your eyes and slowing down your breath. As you do this, you will also be slowing down your brain waves. With each leisurely breath that you take, count backward from ten to one, as you visualize yourself descending on an elevator. See each number displayed in your mind's eye, as you go from one level to the next, until you reach a deeper state of consciousness. Stay aware of your breath, as you slowly inhale and exhale. When you feel that you have achieved a very deep, relaxed state of mind; use your third eye to gaze at the space between your brows. It is very important that you activate the mental screen of your mind in order to create clear pictures. You can begin by consciously projecting images onto your mind's mental screen, starting with simple colors and numbers. In doing so, you are increasing the power of your imagination. This is the language of creation, the language to which the Universe responds.

Everything begins as thought before it materializes. When you learn to slow down your brain waves to obtain the alpha state of mind; you will begin to experience expanded consciousness. This leads to unlimited possibilities and will enable you to enhance and create your life as you want it to be. In addition, you will become more attuned to the thought energy waves and the incoming information that is being impressed on your brain cells from outside sources. These will help to protect you from allowing unwanted negativity into your psychic space.

As "form follows thought", it is in working from the alpha level of mind that you can imagine and manifest the life you desire. The Universe will respond to any thought that is backed by a strong desire, intention, and expectation; as long as it is in alignment for the good of all mankind. The easiest energy to transmit is love. You can send out thoughts of love to create healing for yourself and others.

At the alpha state of consciousness, the mind is very impressionable. When functioning at this level of mind, you can make suggestions and conjure up images of the best version of yourself that you would like to become. You can program your mind for self-improvement in order to lose weight, overcome illness, or break an undesired habit. It is important that you use positive thoughts and imagery only. Rise above fear and don't dwell on negativity. Keep in mind that your thoughts are responsible for creating the prototype for your life.

Once you have had significant time to practice entering the alpha level of mind, you can sharpen your skills by using your mind to project clear pictures of exactly what you want to manifest. For instance, if you want to send healing energy to another person, create a hologram in your mind of complete wholeness and wellness for that person. Do not dwell on, or accentuate any idea of illness. In this way, you begin to build a new paradigm.

When I am engaging in an energy healing session with a client; oftentimes in my mind's eye, I will see a dark cloud over a particular body part. When this happens, I focus light like a laser beam over the area, until I see the dark cloud dissipate. If I see a mass or tumor growth over an area, I send an image of light, melting the tumor and washing it out of the body. At the end of any healing session, I shake or clap my hands, in order to cast out and break up any residual, unwanted energy. Then, I surround the recipient in an orb of pink, glowing, healing light of love and protection.

When you learn to voluntarily enter the alpha state of mind, this opens the door to a realm of infinite possibilities. There are absolutely no limits to what you can achieve. Remember, you can manifest anything that you can imagine, as long as it is in alignment with the good of all.

*"An idea is a being incorporeal, which has no subsistence by itself, but gives figure and form unto shapeless matter, and becomes the cause of the manifestation." - Plutarch*

# Chapter 14
## How to Use Your Mind to Alter Reality

You may wonder how it is possible to influence and change reality, by using only thoughts, imagination, and visualization techniques. The secret lies in learning to interact with the consciousness of the atom. Scientists have discovered that atoms possess qualities of mind and intelligence. Atoms can discriminate, select, choose, attract, and repel. Atoms are the building blocks of all matter. Essentially, everything that exists is built from atoms. When two or more atoms link up, they create a molecule. Molecules interact to form cells. The cells then combine to form tissues; which in turn make up the organs that make up our bodies.

Every atom is a Universe unto itself, a microcosm of the macrocosm. Your body is a Universe made up of atoms. This means that the Universe is inside you, just as you are inside the Universe. You are the Deity of Manifestation for the body that you inhabit.

The atoms in your body respond according to the directives of your thoughts and emotions. Through the medium of your thoughts, you can influence every atom in your body, as well as every atom in the Universe. When you truly grasp this concept, then your work as a healer and conscious co-creator with the Universe begins.

Within you lies the power to consciously influence reality and to heal yourself and others. When you become aware of the profundity of the power of your thoughts, you will gain access to unlimited possibilities. Learning to consciously control, focus, and direct your thoughts, will change your life completely. When you become skilled at implementing manifestation techniques from the alpha state of mind, you will gain confidence that you can fulfill your dreams.

Once you learn how to enter the alpha state of mind at will, and you become comfortable and proficient in using visualization; you will want to develop your own personal, interactive language to converse with the Universe. This will involve adopting a unique set of metaphors and symbols that hold specific meanings for you. Communicating through the use of imagery is the universal, sacred language of the soul. As you build upon this language, you will become more and more adept at interacting with All That Is.

You can manifest anything that you can imagine. Imagination creates the blueprint for Spirit to fill. To begin, it helps to set up a sacred mental space in your mind where you can go to do your psychic work. Once you have established this hallowed place, you will find yourself returning to it over and over again. This is your "Intuitive Workshop", where you can go to gather information psychically, communicate with loved ones over long distances, send healing energy, and initiate any kind of change that you wish to see in the world.

As you construct your inner sanctuary, try to visualize every detail clearly in your mind's eye. Your workspace will need to contain a supernatural tool chest, stocked by your imagination. Using mental imagery, you can begin to gather custom tools to help you perform your healing and manifestation work. Essentially, you will be preparing to perform psychic treatments and surgeries. You will be communicating with atoms, using mental pictograms, to create the future. For example, in your tool chest, you may have an imaginary mop that you can use to mop up excess fluid in the lungs of somebody who is suffering from pneumonia, or you may have a psychic laser beam to zap away unwanted growths or infections. You can conjure up any tool in your mind's eye that you may find useful. With practice, you will learn to use these imaginary tools to create new paradigms to help yourself and others.

You may also want to invite guides and master healers into your workspace and ask that they impress you with their energy and their wisdom. It is also helpful to employ color therapy and invoke different colors to influence healing. You can use whatever images or tools that you can come up with. By means of mental imagery, you will be communicating with the atoms to create change.

When you are ready to go to your inner workspace to initiate a session; you will want to begin by consciously slowing down your brain waves to reach the alpha state of mind. Close your eyes and become aware of your breath as you inhale and exhale slowly. Focus on the space between your brows and gaze at the inner screen of your mind. Count down slowly from ten to one. Project each number onto your mental screen and watch it flash three times. As you count backward, you may also want to envision that you are descending floors on an elevator; with each number and each breath, taking you deeper and deeper into your mind. As you reach the bottom floor of the elevator and step out through the portal that leads to your inner workshop; you may meet a spiritual guide or master healer who is waiting there to assist you.

Once you are very relaxed and satisfied that you have achieved a deeper, more meditative state of mind, it is time to practice developing your third eye vision. When you feel like you are having success at seeing numbers and colors clearly, then you are ready for the next step, which is constructing mental pictures and sending them forth from your mind. With practice, you will become proficient at projecting images onto the inner screen of your mind with clarity and detail. Once you have mastered these visualization techniques, you will be ready to begin your creative work.

There are no fixed rules regarding exactly how you should go about instigating change. The process is unique for every individual. My advice is to begin by projecting an image of your current reality up on the screen of your mind. When you have a clear visual representation before you, mentally use an eraser tool and erase what you don't want to see in your reality. Once your inner canvas is void of all that you don't want, you can visualize a new paradigm. The Universe will respond. Listen for the voice of Spirit and act on any information that you get intuitively. It's coming from the Great Mind of God.

Oftentimes, I take the opportunity to consciously enter the alpha state of mind right before going to sleep at night. As I linger with my eyes closed; I instruct my mind to remain aware, in order to prevent myself from drifting off into a deeper sleep. In the alpha state, I may replay the day in my mind and review the encounters I had. I send out love and light to those who are in need of healing. I also check in with my own body and send healing energy to any part or organ that is experiencing discomfort. I invite my guides, masters, and angels to be with me and to help me with problem-solving. When I am finished setting my intentions and sending healing energy; I seal my work with the declaration, "So Be It". Then, it is time to let go and trust that it is in the hands of the Universe.

*"Be like a tree and let the dead leaves drop."*
*-Rumi*

# Chapter 15
## Rising Above the World of Duality

As souls, we originate from a realm of pure positive love. When we come to this planet, we enter what is sometimes referred to as, "The Valley of Forgetfulness". Our memories are erased as we begin a new life. We forget our Oneness and have no recollection of where we came from or why we are here.

As humans, we live in an illusory world of duality; a world made up of both positive and negative energies. These opposing energies create friction in our lives; setting up conditions and situations that we must work through, in order for our souls to evolve. The physical world is an illusionary world of separateness. In this world of matter, we get the sense that we are disconnected from our Divine Source and from each other. In truth, we are all One. However, we can only know this truth when we are able to rise above our egos and experience our interconnectedness, as a Unified Field of Consciousness.

Oneness is the coming together of all opposites. It is the Divine essence of who we are. When we meditate on the Oneness of all of life, we gain the experience and understanding that we are indeed a part of everything that exists. Every person, every animal, every plant, every insect, every cloud, every sunrise, and every sunset, is a reflection of the same Divine Spirit.

There is no need to fight and struggle with life, for in doing so we only fight against ourselves and the perfect harmony of the Universe. Duality exists in the realm of thoughts. When we are able to grasp the profundity of this concept, we can begin to recognize and transmute the opposing energies that we encounter in our everyday lives, by consciously controlling our thoughts.

As you go about your daily tasks, it's easy to forget who you truly are. If you fall into believing the illusion of separateness and negativity; you will lose your clarity. If you allow yourself to get stuck in the mire of judgments and comparisons; your ego will take you down. To counter the opposing forces that attempt to lead you astray, focus on your heart and remind yourself every day that you are an infinite being, composed of love and light, at one with the Universe.

With this knowledge and assurance, it is up to you to guard against absorbing negative energies that can have a destructive impact on your emotional and physical well-being. In the world of duality, you will find that negativity is everywhere. It floats in the ethers; in clouds made up of thought forms from people who are frustrated, angry, unhappy, and resentful. If you are a sensitive person, you will feel and pick up these energies. You may find that suddenly you experience an unsettled feeling for seemingly no reason at all. When this occurs, you may be subconsciously reacting to negative energy that is being aimed at you from someone who is jealous or engaging in gossip behind your back. Negative energy can accumulate and linger in your aura as unprocessed shame. It can come from the residual pain you still carry from traumas that occurred during childhood.

Trauma at any stage in life can cause great shifts in the way you view yourself and the world. Singular traumatic events have the power to shake you to your core and erode your sense of confidence and self-esteem. If not addressed, these harmful feelings can persist, creating a rippling effect that may plague you over a lifetime.

Negative energy can be contagious. It carries a vibration that is caustic and disturbing. Therefore, it is very important for you to learn to recognize it when it seeps into your life and protect yourself from its influence. It is vital that you stand as a sentinel at the gate of your mind and forbid any negative thoughts to enter. Viewing the world through a negative lens can become habitual. It's easy to get caught up in a loop of thinking that only perpetuates more negativity. If you are not vigilant, and you are a sensitive person, you will tend to absorb the energy around you and take it all in as your own. This can cause depression and illness. For this reason, it is very important to cleanse your mind and your environment energetically on a regular basis.

The first step in clearing negativity from your life is to become aware of what the negativity is and where it is coming from. Become conscious of your self-talk. What is the chatter in your mind saying to you? What thoughts do you find yourself thinking over and over again? You will want to pay close attention to what arises when you begin to observe your own subconscious thoughts. This will give you clues to what is bothering you on the deepest and most internal level of your psyche. Is the voice inside your head telling you repeatedly that nobody likes you, or you'll never be good enough, or worth anything, or that you don't matter? Do you live in a constant state of fear that bad things might happen to you? Are you afraid of being abandoned by somebody you love?

When you are confronted by negative thoughts, rather than believing what your thoughts are telling you and reacting with emotions such as fear, stress, and anxiety; take a moment to step outside of yourself and reflect on where these thoughts might have originated. Whose voice is in your head? Is it your parents, your peers, your teachers or the bullies at school? Try to identify where all of this crazy self-talk is coming from. Once you understand the origin of your thoughts, you can cancel them out and banish them from your mind forever.

As you release the energies that are trapped inside you; this will enable you to let go of all the worn out fears that hold you back in life and are no longer relevant. Remember, much of the energy you carry is not your own. The fears that you allow to invade your psyche can create a sense of paralysis. Fear will hold you hostage and inhibit you from moving forward to fulfill your destiny.

Some fears that people carry are no more than a habitual response to the unknown. We have all developed certain coping mechanisms to protect ourselves from being hurt physically and emotionally. When we perceive something as a threat to our personal well-being; even though it has no basis in truth, we may respond with an instant, knee-jerk reaction to the situation. This hasty reaction can be nothing more than a learned response; adopted subconsciously from a parent, caretaker or another person who once wielded great influence over our lives.

The opposite of fear is love. By focusing on your heart, you allow yourself to be a channel for love, and everything and everyone around you will be touched in a positive manner. When you trust in love, you can transmute negative energy into positive energy. Cancel destructive thoughts from your mind and replace them with creative, constructive thoughts. Always remember that you are God's child. You have the power to create heaven on Earth. Start where you are and send your soul's light out into the world. In return, you will be surrounded and protected by an energy vortex of pure, positive vibrations. This is how you create a sacred life.

One technique you can use to clear negativity from your life is to meditate on the Universe as an Infinite Field of Abundant Love. You will find that when you place your attention on the Great Field of Love and bring the energy of love into every situation; fear and negativity will disappear. Strive to fill your life with positive energy and surround everyone you meet in love and light. Even if you don't agree with somebody, keep in mind that we are all kindred souls on the same journey. We are all One. Unconditional love is the energy that we all seek and long for. It is the energy that frees our souls.

The body is a depository of internalized emotions stored over a lifetime. Any experience that you have, and the way in which you interpret it, will create a data bank of emotion that is recorded in your body. If your perception of an experience is negative, and if the resulting energy isn't processed in a positive way; it may fester in your body and later manifest as a physical symptom of illness or disease.

Any emotion that is unresolved will manifest in the body as an energy blockage. Internalized emotions may take up residence in the spine, the intestines, or the organs. Healing comes in digging up emotions that have been buried and bringing the stories of those emotions to light. This frees the suppression of negative energy and opens the door to healing.

Some emotions are more damaging than others. The most harmful emotions are those that you keep to yourself; emotions such as guilt or shame. When these heavy, dull emotions are allowed to live in your body, they simmer beneath the surface. Eventually, however, as suppressed emotions continue to churn and build up pressure; like a silent volcano, the volcano one day erupts, spewing its toxins into the air. Once these hidden emotions come out into the open, you will finally have a chance to see them for what they are and heal them.

When you hold a grudge against another person, it is like carrying a dark, heavy, weight with you wherever you go. This quickly becomes a tedious chore and hinders your sense of joy. Letting go of past resentments and engaging in the act of forgiveness is crucial to restoring harmony and healing to your life. It is imperative that you forgive yourself for any guilt or shame that you hold inside. You must also forgive any grievance that you hold against another person or group. When you are able to forgive everything, this will free you of any residual negativity from the past. Every time you practice forgiveness, your energy will become lighter and brighter.

In order to be truly free and rise above the world of duality, it is important to remain conscious that you are a being of Oneness and Light. Become aware of how your own energy is affecting the environment around you. Make an effort to spread good vibrations when interacting with others. Tune in to your own voice and listen to the innate power of every word that you speak. Every utterance either serves to create a better world or to break it down. Fill your energy field with love and let it catch fire. It will spread out from your being, and illuminate the world with light.

*"I can see angels sitting on your ears,
polishing trumpets, replacing strings, stretching new skins
on the drums- and gathering wood for the evening's fire.
They danced last night, but you did not hear them."
- Hafiz*

# Chapter 16
## Connect with Your Angels and Spirit Guides

Have you ever had the experience in a time of crisis or great need; that you have called out to the heavens for help, and felt protection and assistance coming unexpectedly from an unknown source? It's like a miracle occurs and help arrives out of nowhere. The only way for you to validate the existence of spiritual helpers in your own life is through personal experience.

I believe that we all have spirit guides and angels who serve as teachers and protectors to support us on our earthly journey. It wasn't until I was rescued in the mineshaft by an unseen, gentle, loving force that I became absolutely certain of their existence. After that incident, I became aware that there are always invisible spiritual helpers by my side. I opened my heart to their presence and welcomed them into my life. The more I reached out to them, the more validation I received, of their willingness to help me. Each time I put out a request for help, the assistance I needed would arrive miraculously, seemingly out of nowhere. Over the years, I have gained more and more confidence that my relationships with my spiritual helpers are ones that I can count on.

In my research on the phenomenon of angels and spirit guides, I have discovered that they are energy beings who walk hand in hand. Angels manifest as a consciousness of pure love energy, connected to the Oneness and the love of the Divine. Spirit guides are souls who have lived a human life before. They understand the illusion of separateness and what it is like to be human. Our guides and angels surround us at all times with a loving presence. They are here to assist and inspire us throughout our lives.

Some spirit guides are with us lifetime after lifetime. Others may show up to help us through a challenging period in our lives, such as a healing crisis. There are also spirit guides who come to help us develop innate gifts such as playing music, writing poetry, or creating art. For example, if you are a visual artist and you are working on a painting, you may have a spirit guide visit you, who excelled in painting during an earthly lifetime. Your spirit guide may come to impress your mind with ideas and assist you in developing your skill.

The secret to establishing a relationship with your spiritual helpers is to take time to tune in and acknowledge their presence in your life. Invite them in and keep your heart open. They have always been with you and they know your soul's journey. As you develop your awareness, you will learn to perceive their presence. You may experience a tingling sensation, or feel an overwhelming sense of love when they are around.

It is up to you to embrace the angels and spirit guides who are working in your life. In order to develop a personal relationship with these benevolent beings, you may want to begin by initiating an inner conversation. One way to establish a connection with your angels and spirit guides is to begin by writing in a journal. Every morning, take time to write a letter of gratitude. Acknowledge their presence and thank them for their assistance. In doing this, you will start to open a channel of communication and build an interpersonal relationship that you can count on.

You can also receive messages from your angels and spirit guides by engaging in a phenomenon known as "automatic writing". In order to do this, it will be necessary to raise your own vibration. This will enable you to intercept their messages. You can accomplish this by taking some deep breaths and becoming meditative. Set your conscious mind aside and focus on the intention that you desire to communicate with your guides and angels. At the top of the page, write a salutation such as, "To My Spirit Guides" or "To My Angels". You may also write down a question or concern that you would like to receive insight on. When you are ready, let the incoming energy move you, as you begin to type or write down, anything that pops into your mind. Don't judge or analyze what you are writing, just let it flow.

When you are finished, go back and read what you have written. You may have an epiphany on how to solve a problem or gain an understanding of what steps you need to take next. Channeled information tends to hold a high vibration and will bring you comfort or clarity. If the writing seems to be heavy in nature, you may be writing from your own emotional body. Intuitive guidance from your spirit guides and angels will hold profound wisdom while feeling light and simply expressed.

In the space of silence, messages from your angels and spirit guides may manifest in subtle ways. A message may be heard as a whisper on the wind or in the gentle fluttering of a butterfly's wings. It is in emptying the mind and becoming silent that you will begin to receive inner guidance. You may get a flash of intuition or a hunch about something, or there may be a message for you in the words of a conversation from a passerby. Be aware and observant of the symbols and metaphors that appear as you go about your daily life. Keep in mind, that from the perspective of a soul living in a physical body, life is a waking dream. This means that everything unfolding around you is potent with messages and lessons. Make it a point to tune in and pay attention to what your angels and spirit guides are trying to show you.

For most of us, our daily lives are full of distractions, noise, and chatter. When we leave the sanctuary of our homes and immerse ourselves in social consciousness; we are met by a society that is absorbed in trivial things, distracted by cell phones and technological devices. We are assaulted by the clamor of traffic, beeps, bells, whistles, radios, and TVs. If you are a sensitive person, you may even be affected by the random thoughts that are flying around in the ethers, as you absorb the energy from the environment around you. When this occurs, your connection with Spirit is challenged and it is easy to forget to focus within and listen to the internal voice. It is easy to get caught up in mundane matters of insignificance and forget who you truly are. When you feel yourself getting sucked into the mire of social chaos and illusion, try to step aside from your personal involvement and observe events from a higher point of view.

Connecting with your angels and spirit guides is a matter of being receptive. They are always with you, as close as your breath. You can meet them in the moment when you become present in the moment. When you take the steps to participate in actively communicating with them, they are able to serve you so much better. Keep your heart and your mind open as you listen to the stillness. The more time you spend in silence, the clearer the voices of your spiritual helpers will become. Move forward in life confidently, knowing that your life is meaningful and you have a host of guides and angels on your side.

When you set out to be a force for good in the world, your power will be magnified a thousand times. Trust that you are on the right path. Trust that you are being guided to connect with the right people, and the Universe is supporting you in all of your endeavors. Trust and expect that doors will open for you.

It is through your own personal experience that you will be able to validate the presence of the spiritual helpers working in your life. Ask and you shall receive! You can ask for help from your spirit guides and angels at any time, for anything. To begin, you may experiment by simply asking for help in finding a parking space. You will be amazed as you drive up to find your perfect parking space waiting for you time after time. Just ask and then trust in the outcome.

Align yourself with the power of the Universe, and walk hand in hand with Spirit. As you begin to engage in conversation with your spiritual helpers, your life will become a living meditation. Miraculous events will become commonplace and occur spontaneously all around you.

"There is more wisdom in your body than
in your deepest philosophies."
-Friedrich Nietzsche

# Chapter 17
## The Conscious Intelligence of the Body

Your body serves as a miraculous machine that sustains you; allowing you to enjoy and experience what it is to be alive. Each cell within your body is intelligent and is in constant communication with other cells by means of hormones and chemical signals.

On a micro-level, the membrane of a cell functions in very much the same way as the brain does. The cell membrane essentially acts as a nervous system. It can see, hear, feel, and interpret the hormonal and chemical messages that are sent through the circulatory system. When these messages are received, and the information is deposited into the hormonal receptors on the surface of the cell; the information is then interpreted and the appropriate substances are created. These substances travel to the cell's nucleus, where the genes in the nucleus receive instructions to synthesize proteins that will perform various functions within the cell. These proteins control and regulate the function of the cells within the rest of the body.

Hormones are made and released by the endocrine glands. The endocrine system is a chemical messenger system that releases hormones directly into the bloodstream. There are six major endocrine glands that serve different purposes. They work together to regulate hormone release and maintain homeostasis in the body.

The hypothalamus is an endocrine gland located in the brain. It serves as the connector between the endocrine and nervous systems and plays an important part in many essential functions of the body. When the hypothalamus receives a signal from the nervous system, it produces hormonal secretions to preserve and maintain the body's internal balance. It is important to note that the messages received by the hypothalamus are oftentimes dictated by the mind's interpretation and perception of outer events. The way in which the mind interprets an event is influenced by an individual's emotional or mental state. In essence, a person's thoughts and attitudes can play an integral part in determining the internal well-being of the body. This is why it is important to have a positive outlook on life and try not to dwell on fear or negativity.

Cortisol is known as the stress hormone. When an individual is under stress or faced with a crisis situation; the adrenal glands release cortisol into the bloodstream, which triggers a fight-or-flight response. This response was originally designed by nature to ensure the survival of man in primitive times; back when mankind was in the hunter-gatherer stage and fighting off wild predators. Today, in modern times, this fight-or-flight mechanism doesn't serve us well at all. As a species, we are no longer running from lions in order to survive. However, our bodies interpret any kind of fear or stress in the same way; sounding the alarm for the adrenal glands to release cortisol into the bloodstream. As a result, the body becomes mobilized and ready for action. When this happens, in order to bring cortisol levels back into balance, there needs to be a reciprocal physical action, such as fighting or running, in order to release the energy of fight-or-flight. If this doesn't occur, cortisol levels build up in the blood and wreak havoc on the body.

Cortisol acts by increasing heart rate, blood pressure, blood glucose, respiration, and muscle tension. It is one of the steroid hormones. Elevated cortisol levels have been known to lower immune function, interfere with memory and learning, decrease bone density, and cause premature aging, weight gain, and heart disease. High levels of cortisol can also cause mental illness and depression by wearing down the brain's ability to function properly. Too much cortisol circulating through the blood is known to kill brain cells and reduce the size of the brain. Cortisol can generate a negative effect on the brain by hardwiring pathways between the hippocampus and the amygdala; thus creating a feedback loop that predisposes the brain to be in a constant state of fight-or-flight. People who suffer from PTSD are especially susceptible to high cortisol levels; as they carry vast amounts of trauma from prior events in their lives that constantly get re-triggered over and over again. Reconciling the energy surrounding these stressful events, and convincing the body that there is no longer a danger, will help to normalize cortisol levels over time.

There are a number of things you can do to combat high cortisol levels. First of all, give yourself permission to relax. Assess the stressors in your life and take steps to minimize stress through exercise, meditation, or comic relief. In order to balance cortisol levels, physical activities like kickboxing or sparring are great ways to recreate the "fight" response and let out aggression without hurting anybody. Other aerobic activities like jogging, swimming, or biking are also good ways to recreate the "flight" outlet and burn up cortisol.

All of the cells in the body are affected and controlled by interactions within the body's internal environment. When a person is in a chronic state of stress, their perceptions and reactions are stored in the cellular memory. Stress hormones create a negative internal reality in the body. On the other hand, if a person lives in stress-free surroundings and has a positive, open, and relaxed outlook on life; this supports a healthy, vibrant internal reality in the body that is stored in the memory of the cells.

Just as we are responsible for creating our outer realities through the thoughts that we think, we are also accountable for our inner realities and the well-being of our physical bodies. As humans, we are the embodiment of energy. Our bodies are sculpted by life's experiences, along with acquired beliefs and mindsets. Every posture has an emotion or mental attitude behind it.

The words that you habitually utter under your breath have a tremendous impact on your physical well-being. The body is made up of approximately fifty trillion cells, and every cell in the body is conscious. It is important to be aware that your body is always listening and responding to every word that you think or speak. Your heart, lungs, kidneys, muscles, blood, and bones are all listening. For this reason, it is important to be conscious of your words and thoughts at all times; making certain that you are nurturing your body with positive images and loving kindness each day.

Take a moment to analyze the self-talk that your body is absorbing, and consequently, responding to. What kind of messages are you sending to your body? Are you sending messages of fear and constantly worrying about coming down with a particular illness? If so, your fearful thoughts are helping to create precisely what it is that you are hoping to avoid. Do you lament about not having certain physical attributes that you perceive would make you more attractive? Do you curse certain physical traits that you inherited from your parents? If you have a chronic ailment or disease, do you coddle its existence by referring to it as something that you possess, using words such as *my* asthma, *my* ulcer, or *my* bad back? When you do this, by taking ownership of it, you are reinforcing the illness in your mind. Do not allow the concept of ill health to take over your consciousness. Instead, focus on strength and wellness.

In any given moment, the body manifests as a portrait of the past. A person's posture may reflect happiness, confidence, and success, or it may mirror the fears and failures that one is holding onto. The health of the body is affected by a person's attitude and feelings of self-worth, as well as their ability to live in gratitude and to forgive the past.

Emotions are simply "energy in motion". It is easy to discern how a person is feeling by the way in which they carry themselves and the energetic aura that surrounds them. Emotions of joy and sadness are written in the expressions and the lines on the face, whereas, feelings of confidence or dejection are reflected in the posture. Every emotion, that one experiences, serves either to build the body up or break it down. Some emotions such as anger, depression, and fear are extremely detrimental to one's health. Positive emotions such as optimism, gratitude, and compassion are known to reinforce physical vitality by having a beneficial effect on the heart and the function of the immune system.

Unprocessed emotions can take up residence in the different organs in the body. Sadness is stored in the lungs, making it difficult for one to breathe fully. Love, or the lack of love in one's life, can either strengthen or weaken the heart. Anger is stored in the liver. Excessive worry can cause stomach ailments or digestive problems. Anxiety affects the spleen, and fear is stored in the kidneys.

In order to send healing energy to a specific organ in the body, you can use the following technique for yourself and others. First, close your eyes and visualize the organ that you would like to heal. Hold a loving resonance towards that organ and see the organ as whole, healthy, and vital. Next, visualize that you are planting a tiny seed of light into that organ. See the light grow and spread throughout the whole body. When you are finished, close the healing session with words of affirmations such as, "So Be It". Then, release it to the Universe.

Another simple visualization that you can do to help strengthen and heal your body is one that can be done in the shower. While standing under the water, visualize that the water pouring over you is actually white light, raining down from the Ocean of Consciousness and Love. Allow the divine healing light to fill your whole body with positive energy, cleansing away all illness and unwanted density. See the light in your mind's eye, filling and pulsing through your veins, and spreading to every organ. In affirmation, give thanks to Spirit for your own good health and for sustaining your life.

The body has its own remarkable intelligence and constantly strives to heal itself and maintain its own ultimate vitality. The human body is truly a temple to be honored with deep and profound gratitude. In addition to following the advise of your doctor or health professional, you can take care of your body by eating nourishing food, drinking clean, pure water, and breathing in fresh, unpolluted air. When you send love and appreciation to your body, and all of its organs and parts, the body will receive this energetically and respond accordingly.

*"Forgive others, not because
they deserve forgiveness,
but because you deserve peace."
- Buddha*

# Chapter 18
# Self-Love and the Freedom of Forgiveness

Forgiveness is a gift that you give to yourself. Whether you have been injured emotionally or physically by another person or event, you will never be able to heal completely until you are able to find forgiveness in your heart. When you remain entangled in old energetic cords of resentment, it keeps you bound to the pain and the people who have hurt you. This drains your energy and prevents you from rising to your full potential.

In order to envision and embrace a new life for yourself, it is absolutely necessary that you make peace with your past. Forgive every person who has ever done you wrong, and let go of the memories of all disturbing events that still plague you. In addition, forgive yourself for everything you feel guilty about or blame yourself for.

At times, you may feel that you could have done better or should have done better in certain situations, but you have to let it go and accept that you did the best you could for your stage of development at that time in your life. Be gentle with yourself. Keep in mind that your mission on Earth is to grow in awareness and to learn from your experiences. Leave the past behind, but take the lessons with you to create a better future.

Perhaps there is someone in your past who picked on you or abused you, and to this day, you are still unable to let go of the grudge that you hold against them. You may catch yourself replaying all of the details about what happened, over and over in your mind.

When you do this, you are defeating yourself by keeping the pain of past trauma alive. You are allowing that person to remain in your present life and persistently punish you again and again. You hand over your power to memories that continue to upset you. The truth is that the past is behind you, and the person whom you still hold a grudge against probably moved on a long time ago. Most likely, that person has completely forgotten the incident, yet somehow you remain stuck; looping through the scenario over and over again in your mind, ruminating about how unfair you were treated and how angry you still are. When you can't let the past go and are unable to come to a place of peace and forgiveness in your heart; you will continue to be tormented. This prevents you from focusing on the present moment and living your life fully today.

Do not let the past define your destiny. Do not allow these attacks on your spirit to hinder your progress in achieving your soul's dream for you. Everything that was once a source of suffering can become a catalyst for your spiritual growth. When you are willing to forgive, you open the door to set your spirit free.

All of us have experienced painful situations that left us with deep, emotional scars. Every experience from the past leaves an energetic imprint on the nervous system. These energies are reawakened when triggered by events that conjure up old feelings from previous traumas. When you have an unsettled feeling inside, it can be an indication that you are wrestling with unprocessed emotions that are still tormenting you. The residual energy from a distressing past event is continuing to show up in your daily life and rob you of your happiness. It is only when you take the steps to identify and dissipate painful memories that you will experience inner peace. Summon up the courage to face your own darkness, for you can only be free when you are no longer afraid of the dark.

Sometimes, when people and situations in your current life resemble people and situations from the past, it can cause stressful memories to be reactivated. All of a sudden, you may find yourself reliving in your mind, disturbing events that you thought you left behind. You might begin to experience the old feelings that were attached to those incidences all over again. When this happens, it's easy to fall into old patterns and behaviors, and revert back to coping mechanisms that ultimately leave you feeling socially alienated and alone. In order to prevent this from happening, there needs to be a conscious effort on your part, to be preemptive in recognizing and avoiding the pitfalls of the past. Your previous perceptions of what has gone before can stir up hurtful memories and bring them into the present. To avoid becoming trapped, it is important to focus on the moment at hand and strive to see things in a new light. Remember, you are the creator of your reality now.

Negative energies from the past can also linger in the body, causing pain, discomfort, and disease. A person, who has been bullied or mistreated as a child, may respond by developing a posture of armor for protection. This is an attempt to shield the heart. Oftentimes, it is easy to identify what one's past has been like, just by looking at a person's posture. You can tell if someone is feeling confident or defeated. The past is reflected in how a person moves, as well as in everything a person says and does.

Self-love and forgiveness are absolutely essential to your physical and mental well-being. All of the self-deprecating thoughts and defeating behaviors that you engage in can be traced back to issues stemming from lack of self-love. The guilt that you hold onto from the past can become a cesspool that seems nearly impossible to crawl out of. Try your best to uncover the beliefs that lurk in your subconscious mind. Acknowledge the residual feelings of guilt and shame, and the holding patterns in your body that are associated with painful memories. Unless you are able to forgive and let go, the pain that you carry from your past will continue to have an effect on your physical and mental well-being.

Many of us have grown up in less than ideal circumstances. Whatever happened in the past, whether we suffered from abuse, neglect, bullying, sexual molestation, or mistreatment from an alcoholic or addicted parent; every experience left an impact of how we feel about our own self-worth. When children are treated with love and acceptance, they will thrive and feel confident in life. When a child is treated with resentment, that child will retreat into a lonely, protective shell. This is a root cause of depression that can persist over a lifetime and leave deep scars on one's psyche.

I have discovered that in order to forgive and heal the past, it is essential to go back to the very beginning before the wounding occurred, to retrieve and restore the pure seed of shining light within. In a way, it is necessary to metaphorically give birth to yourself all over again; to welcome, love, and nurture the infant that you were when you first came to Earth, as a being of radiant light, with a gift and a purpose to share. It is time for you to reconcile and retrieve your light being. You can go back, transcending time and space, and reach out to heal the inner child who was left behind. It is time to coax this child out of hiding and find the way back to joy and self-love.

Make a promise to honor and treat yourself just as you would love and protect your own precious child. If you consider the circumstances of your life today, as if you were a parent caring for a child; what changes would you make in order to nurture the soul of that child? You are that child.

Consider and identify the relationships with others that do not nurture your inner child's well-being. Are there emotional bullies that your inner child tends to hang out with? As a parent, would you allow this for your own child? If the answer is no, then don't allow it for yourself. Purge your life of any involvement with toxic people. Set the intention that you will only allow people into your life who enter with love and kindness, and have your best interests in mind. The way to attract people into your life, who you truly resonate with, is to make sure that in all situations you are being yourself and coming from your heart.

In order to cope and attempt to feel safe in a hostile world, many of us have allowed ourselves to shrink down to mediocrity. We make ourselves small to avoid being seen or scrutinized. Sadly, the complex dynamics of human interactions, oftentimes seek to attack and diminish others. Many of us hold onto past traumas where we have been shamed, rejected or punished, just for being ourselves. In response, we turn down our inner light and allow our spirits to become dim, so as not to be noticed or challenged.

The mind will automatically believe whatever it hears or absorbs from others, without even considering if it's true or not. Therefore, it is vital to recognize and delete any criticism from your life's record that has had a negative effect on you. Criticism usually comes from a person who is bored, frustrated, and unfulfilled. Look at all of the scenarios that have played out in your life where you have been criticized and felt like you could never measure up. Consider the source of criticism. It says much more about the critic than it says about you. It is time now to sort through what is true and what isn't. It is time to move forward and take your life back. You have the power to make things right. Love yourself, forgive everything, leave the darkness behind and come into the light.

People will only be able to love you to the degree that they are able to love themselves. It is important to remember this, as you seek to understand what the motive behind another person's behavior might be when they attempt to take you down. Sometimes people are just plain unhappy in their lives, and because they are miserable, they want others to be miserable as well. Sometimes people are just jealous. You may represent something or resemble somebody that triggers a painful memory for another person. People will perceive you through the lens of their own past experiences; therefore, you may be the subject of unfair judgments. It is vital to remember that when someone has an issue against you, it most often has nothing to do with you, but rather it is indicative of how that person perceives the world.

Through no fault of your own, you may become the scapegoat or the psychic punching bag for another person's misgivings. You may be falsely blamed for something you never did. If you are a sensitive person, you quickly pick up on the energetic thoughts that are being directed towards you. If left unchecked, these rogue, destructive energies will enter your mind, take up residence, and eat away at your self-esteem. It is important not to let the toxicity of these energetic thorns get the best of you.

Nurturing self-love is a process of getting rid of all of the psychic barbs that have been placed into your being. Any unresolved memory or emotion can fester inside, causing distress and disease. Now is the time to acknowledge and release all of the guilt and shame that has piled up over the years. It is time to uncover and fall in love with who you truly are; a unique expression of the Divine, a manifestation of God's love.

Ask yourself and then answer the following questions. What are your deepest feelings toward yourself? Are you blaming yourself for something? Are you feeling guilty or ashamed of past actions? Do you think of yourself as inadequate? Take a moment to examine where these notions originally came from.

To forgive another person is not easy. When somebody has betrayed you, forgiving them can be one of the hardest things to do. The only way to truly forgive another person is to rise above your ego. It is the ego that insists on holding onto judgments and keeping score. Be willing to let go of "being right" in exchange for inner peace. This is the freedom of forgiveness.

Our time on Earth is like fleeting sunlight. There isn't a moment to waste carrying clouds of regret. Let it all go. Step into the light and rise above the melancholy worlds of the ego. True healing begins with forgiveness. It begins with you. In forgiving others, you liberate your soul.

*"Be the energy you want others to absorb."*
*-A.D. Posey*

# Chapter 19
## Energetic Healing for Yourself and Others

We are all endowed with inherent healing capabilities. As interconnected beings of energy, light, consciousness, and love; each one of us has an innate ability to interact with the Universal Life Force and to serve as a conduit for healing energy to flow through. The principle of energetic healing lies in the notion that we are all connected in a unified energetic field of consciousness, also known as, The Mind of God. It is through this vast, energetic web of unlimited potentiality that we are able to link in consciousness to create new paradigms.

All form is comprised of energy. This includes everything from planetary systems, all the way down to the tiniest atom. Energy is fluid and malleable and responds to thoughts, emotions, and vibrations. By envisioning what we desire, we can create an ethereal blueprint for the Universe to fill. This gives us the power to influence and change reality. When we learn to tap into the unified energetic field of consciousness; we can create anything that we can imagine. We can generate healing images in our minds and send that healing energy out across the Universe.

You can facilitate healing for another person when you attune your sensitivity and become aware of the subtle energies moving through you. This unlimited energy is a gift from the Universe. Using the power of your mind, combined with the power of your heart; you can direct this stream of energy, with intention, to help and heal others.

Healing is the return of the memory to holiness and reaffirming one's identity as unlimited soul consciousness. Whether someone is dealing with a physical, spiritual, or emotional issue; when a person becomes ill, it is an indication that something is out of balance on some level. Every illness has a root cause. Oftentimes, illness can be traced to stuck patterns of thinking and misguided beliefs that have created energy blockages in the body. If someone is engaging in a tug-o-war between the urge of their soul and the blind will of their ego, they are not living in alignment with their soul's purpose. If someone is shaping their life in order to please others and not living their own truth, that person may be faced with a deep internal conflict that may eventually manifest as a physical ailment.

In an effort to cope with life's struggles, an individual may subconsciously allow a disease to take hold in their body because, for some reason, it serves a particular purpose. For example, a person may need rest, yet their lifestyle does not allow them to take time out. As a result, they may yield to an illness in order for the body to get the rest and rejuvenation it needs. Another example would be if a child is craving attention from a parent, that child may come down with an illness in order to fill a need for love and affection. People might also become sick when they are trying to avoid something in their lives. Illness can be viewed as a way out of a situation that feels threatening or hopeless.

Healing is decided by all consciousness involved. This includes the healer and the person who is receiving the healing. You will only be able to facilitate healing for someone if they have a genuine desire to be healed. If you look deep into the subconscious mind of a person, you may be able to identify an aspect in their life that is leading to poor health. Sometimes, a person who has become sick has also become apathetic about living life. Something is being rejected, which in turn, manifests in the form of a symptom or illness. One of the keys to good health is to have a true desire to be fully alive, and to live in gratitude and appreciation for all that life has to offer.

Many clues to the origin of an illness may be derived in observing the symptoms that a person displays and the part of the body that is affected. For instance, if someone is prone to sore throats; there may be something bothering them that's been left unsaid, or they may have trouble speaking up for themselves. If somebody is grieving from a loss, and experiencing the feeling of a broken heart; this may manifest in the body as heart disease or a disorder involving the heart. If a person doesn't feel like they have the support of others, they may experience hip or leg problems.

In order to enjoy perfect health and vitality of spirit, it is very important to identify and deal with underlying emotions. In seeking to determine the source of an illness, consider how a person's emotional life might be affecting their well-being. When somebody conceals or denies their true feelings, rather than acknowledging them; the suppressed emotional energy may show up elsewhere in the body as "dis-ease". Emotions of sadness and grief can manifest as a weakness in the lungs, whereas the emotion of anger is held in the liver. Worry can cause stomach ailments, and fear can have an effect on the kidneys. All of these negative emotions need to be uncovered and brought to the light, in order to be resolved.

Food also plays a very critical role in maintaining good health. Like everything else, food is made up of energy and vibration. The vibration of the food we eat is absorbed into our bodies. Natural, organic foods are the healthiest foods we can choose to consume. In today's world, much of the food that is available to us is either highly processed or heavily sprayed with pesticides. Many pesticides are made from endocrine-disrupting chemicals. Diseases such as cancer, allergies, neurological disorders, and reproductive disorders have all been linked to pesticide exposure. Our bodies are not designed to deal with the harmful chemicals that are in our food, air, and water supplies. In order to ensure good health, it's important that we limit our exposure to dangerous, life-threatening chemicals, and nourish ourselves with life-affirming foods and pure water. We need to do everything we can to take care of our health, for our bodies make this sacred journey of life possible.

You can help to heal yourself and others when you truly believe in your power to alter reality through the unified energy field. Be willing to allow the healing energy of the Universe to flow through you. Hold love in your heart and offer yourself as an open channel for the river of God to reach into this world. In the spirit of compassion, listen to your inner voice and let the love be your guide.

## Healing Meditation

Close your eyes and think of the person who is in need of healing as a hologram. Connect to this hologram with love in your heart and affirm perfect wellness in your mind's eye. Visualize this hologram as a perfect, divine blueprint of the body. Wipe away any shadows or blocks that you may see. These blocks are manifestations of suppressed emotions and the places where one has become stuck. Dark clouds indicate organs and other parts of the body that need energy. To restore the light in the body, imagine that your own body is a river of light and you are an open channel. Allow the healing light to fill your being. This light will heal you as it flows through you, and continues to stream out into the world. With love in your heart, you can send this river of energy to others, simply by holding them in consciousness. In your mind's eye, see and affirm that the person you are sending healing energy to, is completely whole and healthy. Give thanks and release it to the Universe.

*"You have no need to travel anywhere.*
*Journey within yourself,*
*Enter a mine of rubies and bathe*
*in the splendor of your own Light."*
*—Rumi*

# Chapter 20
## Understanding Chakras, Auras, and the Light Body

Every living thing is surrounded by an energy field of light. This energy field is called an aura. The human aura surrounds the body in a protective, interactive, luminous sheath. It consists of shifting waves of light that fluctuate with different colors and intensity. The patterns of light that appear in the aura reflect the quality of one's health, mood, and well-being at any particular moment in time. Whatever shows up in the physical body is revealed in the aura first. This field of light is an expanded version of who we are.

There are seven layers in the human aura. Each layer is associated with one of the seven major chakras. The layers of the aura consist of energetic emanations from the physical body, as well as emanations from the higher-frequency, subtle bodies such as; the astral, mental, causal, etheric, and soul bodies.

The aura serves as a defense mechanism to protect and prevent unwanted energies from entering one's psychic space. Harmful energies may enter as negative thought forms that are directed towards a person by someone who is jealous or has malicious intentions. The aura, also known as the human energy shield, can be strengthened by meditation, visualization, yoga, and positive affirmations. On the other hand, stressful events or the use of drugs and alcohol can weaken the aura and leave holes in the auric field. This allows harmful, negative, and predatory energies to enter, which can drain a person's vitality.

The aura is constantly changing, moment to moment, according to how a person is feeling at the time. It is a good indicator of an individual's disposition and state of health. Happy, healthy people have strong, bright auras, whereas people who are sick or emotionally distraught, have weak shadowy auras.

When two people share a deep emotional bond, their auras may merge into one another, thus creating a shared aura. This often occurs in close relationships; such as relations between couples, parents and children, siblings, twins, and even best friends. Whenever two or more people share a close connection and there is a physical or emotional separation; it can be very difficult for the people involved to adjust. They will be left with the feeling that something is missing in their lives. This is the reason why it can be so difficult to recover after a breakup or the death of a loved one. When two auras separate from one another, a void is created that takes time to heal.

Anybody can learn to see and read auras with a little practice. The dominant colors in a person's aura may indicate where someone has become obsessed or fixated. Different colors in the aura also indicate general tendencies or areas of interest. For example, when the color blue shows up in an aura, it relates to the throat chakra. A person, who has a great deal of blue in their aura, might be a writer or a speaker. The color red is associated with the root chakra, which is related to physical activity. Athletes tend to have a lot of red in their auras. The colors green and pink are often observed in the auras of people who are healers. Both colors are associated with the heart chakra.

In order to get a sense of a person's character, even before you attempt to read their aura, you can obtain clues by taking notice of the color of clothing they are wearing. You can also get a clue about the predominant colors in a person's aura by asking them what their favorite color is. This will give you insight into a person's personality and their focus in life. Each color carries its own particular vibration and has specific characteristics.

The colors that show up in the aura reflect the colors of the chakra centers. In Sanskrit, the word chakra means wheel. Chakras are swirling, energetic points of light, where lines of energy cross. There are seven major chakras. Each chakra corresponds to a different point along the spine and is connected to a major organ. It is through the chakras that we are connected to the Universal Life Force. The colors of the chakras are arranged just like the seven colors of the rainbow or the colors of a prism. In chronological order, they are red, orange, yellow, green, blue, indigo, and violet.

The first chakra, referred to as the "root chakra" or "base chakra", is located at the base of the spine. The color associated with this chakra is red. The root chakra establishes the connection of the physical body to the earth. It is a grounding force that carries the energy of survival and getting one's physical needs met. The first chakra is responsible for providing a sense of safety and security on this earthly journey. It is the most instinctual of all of the chakras. The fight-or-flight response is initiated from this chakra and reflects the primal, animalistic nature of man. The energy of the root chakra inspires a person to be courageous and resourceful and activates the will to survive during times of adversity. The root chakra is also known to carry ancestral memories. It is widely believed that ancestral memories of events that threatened the survival of our ancestors, such as war, famine, and natural disasters, are recorded in the subtle bodies and imprinted in the energies of the first chakra. These ancestral memories are passed down from generation to generation, to ensure the survival of future generations. If this is indeed true, it explains why so many people face challenges in the root chakra. A blockage in the root chakra may manifest emotionally as anger or violence, or a person may have the feeling of being ungrounded, abandoned, worried, or anxious. On a physical level, the root chakra primarily governs the lower extremities; including the pelvic floor, the legs, and the feet.

The second chakra is also known as the "sacral chakra". It is located in the lower abdomen, just below the navel and above the pubic bone. This is where the inner child resides and is known to be the center of pleasure, enjoyment, and creativity. The sacral chakra is also referred to as "the seat of emotions". Suppressed emotions and energy from traumatic life events are stored in the second chakra. This includes feelings associated with being accepted or rejected, and experiences encompassing love and hate. The second chakra is related to pleasure, sexuality, and reproduction. The color associated with this chakra is orange. When the sacral chakra is balanced, an individual will experience feelings of wellness, abundance, pleasure, and joy. The energy of the second chakra encourages one to let go and play like a child. A blockage in the sacral chakra may lead to addictions, depression, repressed emotions, sexual guilt, and lack of creative energy. Health issues that may arise from an imbalance in the second chakra include disorders of the spleen, kidneys, the urinary system, and the reproductive organs. Symptoms may include sexual dysfunction, sciatica, chronic lower back pain, as well as a loss of interest in sensual pleasures.

The third chakra, which is also referred to as the "solar plexus", is located just above the navel, in the upper part of the belly where the diaphragm rests. This chakra is where one possesses a sense of strength, confidence, and personal power in the world. It is characterized by the expression of free will, taking responsibility for one's life, making decisions, setting a course of action, self-discipline, and independence. The color associated with the third chakra is yellow. This chakra is closely connected to the digestive system. Its main function is to help transform matter into energy to fuel the body. It governs metabolism and is associated with the pancreas. A blockage in the third chakra may manifest emotionally as a sense of victimization. There may also be issues involving lack of self-confidence, lack of purpose or ambition, fear, anxiety, or feelings of helplessness. Health issues associated with an imbalance in the third chakra may include eating disorders such as anorexia and bulimia, indigestion, ulcers, pancreatitis, diabetes, adrenal fatigue, gallbladder and liver disorders, and intestinal dysfunction.

The fourth chakra is the "heart chakra". It is located in the center of the chest. It is through this chakra that the energy of love finds its way into the world. It is from the heart chakra that the love we feel for others originates. The colors associated with the heart chakra are green and light pink. The energy that emanates from this chakra is healing, loving, gentle, and compassionate. The fourth chakra connects the lower and upper chakras; and acts as the point of integration of earthly matters and higher, spiritual aspirations. If somebody is experiencing a blockage in this chakra, it may manifest physically as a problem with the heart, the circulatory system, or the immune system. One may also experience frequent asthma attacks, or other lung problems, as well as problems with the shoulders and upper back. Emotionally painful events such as rejection, abuse, grief, trauma or loss, can leave an energetic imprint on the heart chakra. A person with an emotional blockage in the heart chakra may display resentment, bitterness, grief, anger, self-centeredness, jealousy, lack of compassion, and an inability to trust others. There may also be a tendency for one to withdraw from society and to become isolated. In order to heal the heart chakra, it is important to focus on self-love, forgiveness, and releasing the pain caused by unhealed relationships.

The fifth chakra is the "throat chakra". Located at the center of the neck at the level of the throat, this is the center for creativity, communication, music, speaking, and writing. The color associated with this chakra is blue. The throat chakra is where we summon up the energy to share our creativity and to speak our truth. It is the place of will, expression, and control. The throat chakra controls the thyroid gland and the endocrine system. It is responsible for the regulation of the flow of hormones and all matters pertaining to the throat and the head. A blockage in the throat chakra occurs when one is not able to communicate their emotions fully, and as a result, they become shut down. This may result in extreme shyness that limits a person's ability to communicate effectively, for fear of ridicule and judgment from others. Non-physical symptoms that may manifest as a result of a blocked throat chakra may include a fear of speaking, or an inability to express one's thoughts. A person may also develop extreme social anxiety. Physical symptoms of a blocked fifth chakra may include chronic sore throats, tonsillitis, hoarseness, laryngitis, difficulty swallowing, thyroid issues, mouth ulcers, problems with the tongue, dental issues, tinnitus, TMJ, neck pain, and difficulty eating. In order to heal the throat chakra, it is important to be willing to let go of the past and to work on expressing oneself honestly, in a heartfelt way, without holding back. This may include speaking openly and honestly with friends and family or writing down feelings in a journal without censorship. Singing helps to dispel blockages of the throat chakra by getting the energy flowing through sound and vibration. Having a good cry can also help to heal and balance the throat center. The key to restoring the energy balance of the fifth chakra is to be honest with one's feelings while working through and releasing past guilt, hurt, and resentment.

The sixth chakra, also known as the "third eye chakra", is located in the brain at the point between the brows. The color associated with the sixth chakra is indigo. It is traditionally associated with the pituitary gland. The third eye chakra gives one the ability to visualize and to see both the inner and outer worlds. It is considered to be the seat of intuition and wisdom. When one gazes through the third eye in meditation, it opens the door to accessing inner guidance to see deeper truths. From this center, one is guided by visions that illuminate the path to creating life consciously. The sixth chakra is associated with clairvoyance, psychic abilities, imagination, and dreaming. It is also associated with celestial love, extending compassion to all of life, and loving unconditionally. When the sixth chakra becomes blocked, a person may experience physical symptoms such as migraine headaches, sinusitis, seizures, or poor vision. Emotional symptoms resulting from a blockage in the sixth chakra may manifest as anxiety, depression, paranoia, delusions, or sleep difficulties. In order to heal this chakra, it helps to meditate on empathy and forgiveness.

The seventh chakra is the "crown chakra". It is associated with the pineal gland. Located at the top of the head, it is the source of enlightenment and spiritual connection. This chakra helps to liberate the soul. It is known as the gateway to the divine self and the link to Universal Consciousness; where one comes to recognize their own being as pure awareness. It is through the seventh chakra that the river of God rushes in to fill a person with spiritual light. This chakra helps one to transcend the ego and to experience unity with every living thing on this planet. It is the meeting point between the finite and the infinite; where the physical and spiritual parts of one's being are integrated. The color associated with this chakra is violet. When a person encounters extreme negativity in the world, it can throw the crown chakra into an imbalanced state. An impairment in the seventh chakra leads to spiritual distress and the false perception that life has no meaning. This may leave one feeling spiritually disconnected, lonely, or isolated, with an inability to connect with others. Physical symptoms that may appear as a result of a crown chakra being blocked include neurological disorders, dementia, frequent headaches, schizophrenia, delusional disorders, and depression. Regular meditation or prayer is very important in helping to open and heal the crown chakra. Visualizing and connecting with the brilliant violet light as it pours into the top of the head will help to wash away any blockages and restore faith in the flow of the Universe.

The first, second, and third chakras are referred to as the lower chakras. The energies of these lower chakras are oriented towards the physical world. The fourth, fifth, sixth and seventh chakras are considered the higher chakras and are oriented towards the spiritual and subtle worlds.

A blocked chakra can often be the cause of health or emotional issues. To heal means to bring the chakras into alignment. In order to strengthen and expand one's own energy field, it is important to focus attention on the chakras. This can be done easily using the "Color Breathing Meditation". The color of each chakra has its own spiritually nourishing quality. It is important to breathe in each color deeply, in order to enlighten and stimulate each chakra energy center.

## Color Breathing Meditation

Sit with your spine aligned. Relax and close your eyes. Start by visualizing the first chakra at the base of the sacrum as a red, spinning wheel of light. Inhale fully and send a deep breath into the root chakra. Allow the red color to activate and circulate throughout your body. As you do this, you will be filled with an energetic current of revitalizing life force that will help to invigorate and strengthen your physical body. The root chakra governs the spinal column, the feet, hips, and legs. The endocrine glands related to the root chakra are the adrenal cortex glands.

Next, focus your attention just below the navel and visualize your second chakra as a spinning wheel of orange light at the sacral center. Breathe in the orange light fully, allowing it to activate the emotional and pleasure center. If you come upon any resistance in this exercise, try to identify if there is an emotional issue bothering you that needs to be resolved. As you allow the orange light energy to circulate throughout your body, center your thoughts on forgiveness and strive to let go of all emotional trauma from past events. Breathe in and out, slowly and deeply, focusing on a feeling of peace within yourself. The sacral chakra governs the reproductive system, the spleen, the bladder, the kidneys, and the lumbar region of the spine. The endocrine glands associated with the second chakra are the gonads.

Next, visualize your third chakra as a vibrating, spinning wheel of yellow light at the solar plexus, just above the navel. This is your power center. As you breathe in the yellow light, allowing it to energize your whole body, contemplate on any fears or anxieties that are holding you back from realizing your dreams. Allow the yellow light to vaporize and dissipate your fears. The third chakra governs the stomach, liver, gallbladder and the nervous system. The endocrine gland associated with this chakra is the pancreas.

Move your attention now to your heart center, the fourth chakra. Visualize your heart chakra as a spinning wheel of green light. Breathe in the green light and let it circulate throughout your whole body. Meditate on love as you breathe in and out. With each breath, expand your heart and send the energy of love out to the Universe. The areas of the body governed by the heart chakra are the heart, the immune system, the blood, and the circulatory system. The endocrine gland associated with the heart chakra is the thymus gland.

Next, place your attention on the throat chakra. In your mind's eye, visualize a magnificent spinning wheel of sparkling blue light. Breathe in the blue light deeply and allow it to circulate throughout your whole body. Meditate on giving yourself the freedom to speak your truth without fear. Give yourself permission to release your creativity into the world. The areas of the body governed by the fifth chakra are the throat, the vocal cords, the mouth, the tongue, the esophagus, and the lungs. The endocrine gland associated with the throat chakra is the thyroid gland.

Next, move your attention to the point between your brows. This is the sixth chakra, also known as the third eye chakra. Visualize a spinning wheel of beautiful indigo light. Allow this light to circulate throughout your body. As you breathe in and out, focus on your third eye. Pay attention to any inner visions that may appear in your mind's eye. This is the center for dreaming, imagination, clairvoyance and psychic ability. The areas of the body governed by the sixth chakra are the brain, eyes, ears, nose, and the nervous system. The endocrine glands associated with this chakra include the pituitary gland and the hypothalamus gland.

Next, move your attention to the seventh chakra located at the top of your head. This is the crown chakra. Visualize a brilliant violet spinning wheel of light. Breathe in the violet light deeply. Meditate on your spiritual connection to the Creative Source of All, and allow that infinite energy to fill and circulate throughout your whole body. The area of the body that is governed by the seventh chakra is the upper brain. The endocrine gland associated with this chakra is the pineal gland.

Located somewhere between four to twelve inches above your head is the highest crown chakra. It is known as the "soul star". The soul star is associated with your soul's purpose. When your soul star is balanced, this will give you a clear sense of purpose and an understanding as to why you have chosen this incarnation. The color associated with the highest crown chakra is white. Visualize a spinning wheel of white light above your head. Breathe in the white light and allow it to fill and circulate throughout your whole body.

Finish the meditation by visualizing all of the chakras from the base of your spine to the highest crown. See in your mind's eye how the chakras are aligned perfectly and spinning with vibrant colors. When your chakras are aligned and expanded, you will feel more balanced and everything will flow more easily.

*"I wish I could show you,
when you are lonely or in darkness,
the astonishing light of your own being."
-Hafiz*

# Chapter 21
## How to See and Read Auras

Everything has an aura; an electromagnetic energy field, made up of varying vibrations and frequencies, which surrounds all living and non-living things. This includes the Earth, the Sun, the Moon, and all of the planets. Everything that is comprised of atoms emanates an energy field, and all of matter is made up of atoms. Within each atom, there is an originating pulse of energy that is set into motion by protons and electrons whirling around the nucleus. The rate of revolution determines one's personal vibration.

The energetic frequency of an individual can be seen in the aura that surrounds them, in waves of color that shift and flow. The intensity of a person's aura varies, according to the quality of energy that radiates from within their being, at any given moment. The human aura contains layers of physical, emotional, mental, and spiritual elements that vibrate at different frequencies. These layers are linked to the subtle bodies.

All of the colors in the rainbow can be found in the aura. The colors in the human aura correspond to the seven chakra centers and reflect one's physical, emotional, mental, and spiritual health. The colors shift and change according to how a person is feeling at the moment. Bright colors indicate that a person is feeling alive and energetic; whereas, dull, muddy colors indicate that a person might be struggling with depression, physical challenges, or energy blockages in the body. The aura is a barometer of one's well-being. Happy, loving thoughts expand the aura; whereas sad, angry, or fearful thoughts cause the aura to contract.

## How to Sense Your Own Energy Field

Learning to see and read auras is easy, once you develop an awareness of the presence of energy that surrounds everything. Here is a simple exercise that will help you to experience the existence of your own energy field.

Close your eyes and begin to rub your hands together vigorously, in order to generate heat. Next, with the palms of your hands open and facing each other, bring your hands together very slowly. As you do this, feel for the energy between your palms. There will be a point where you will feel a warm cushion of energy. This happens, typically when the hands are about one to two inches apart. The energy cushion will feel tangible. You can play with it by pushing your hands together and pulling them apart. As you do this, you will be feeling your own auric field.

Once you get a sense of what the cushion of energy between the palms of your hands feels like, the next step is to begin to scan your own body's energy field. With conscious intention, hold your hand a couple of inches away from your skin and slowly move your hand over all of the parts of your body, including the organs. As you do this, locate the cushion of energy and notice the temperature variations that you feel as you pass your palm over the different areas. When you come to a place that feels noticeably colder, it indicates that there is not much energy flowing to that particular part of the body. The associated organ may be blocked or not functioning in an optimal manner. The areas of the body where you detect excessive heat may indicate places of inflammation or sites where a prior injury has occurred.

As you gain confidence in scanning and sensing your own auric field, you may want to practice scanning the energy fields of your friends or even your pets. Aura scanning is a preliminary diagnostic tool that you can use to assess the overall health and welfare of another living being. The more you practice, the more sensitive your hands will become.

## Eye Fixation Technique

Here is an exercise, known as the "Eye Fixation Technique" that will help you learn to see auras. You will need some sheets of fluorescent-colored paper in different colors; such as fluorescent pink, green, blue, and yellow. You will also need a partner to assist you. Locate a place where you can gaze at a large white surface, such as a white colored board or a white wall. It will be helpful to mark the center of the surface with a piece of masking tape.

When you are ready to begin, take some slow, deep breaths; making sure that you exhale fully with each breath. Then, when you feel like you are in a relaxed state of mind, focus your eyes on the marked spot of the white surface. As you fixate your eyes, ask your partner to hold up a colored piece of paper over the spot where you are gazing. Take a deep breath and as you exhale, imagine that you are moving towards the colored paper. Continue to fixate your eyes and gaze at the fluorescent sheet of paper. When you are ready, ask your partner to remove the paper quickly as you continue to gaze at the white surface. What do you see? You should be able to see the residue of the complementary color left behind. If you are gazing at a florescent-green piece of paper, you should see the residue of the complementary color, red. If you are gazing at a florescent-yellow piece of paper, you should see violet, and if you are gazing at a florescent-blue piece of paper, you should see an orange-colored residue on the white background. This gazing technique will help you to begin to see energetic imprints. When you are able to do this easily, you will be ready to apply this eye fixation technique to actually see auras and energy fields.

In order to practice seeing the human aura, ask your partner to stand in front of a white, or light, neutral-colored background. Become meditative and gaze at your partner's third eye. As you fixate your eyes, take a deep breath and imagine that you are moving towards your partner. Continue to breathe and take in their energy. As you keep your eyes fixated, include the area around your partner's image in your stare. Next, ask your partner to move away from the wall quickly, as you continue to keep your eyes fixed on the spot where your partner just stood. You will see a very quick impression of color flicker on the wall. What you are seeing is the energetic residue of your partner's aura. You must be quick in order to catch a glimpse of it. Take notice of the predominant colors that you observe and pay close attention to where they are placed in regard to the silhouette impression of the body. You may also see other colors flashing through the aura, like bolts of colored lightning.

Try to create a picture in your mind's eye of what you just witnessed. In order to study the aura more thoroughly, use a tablet and colored pencils to create a picture of the aura that you just observed. This will serve as a reference for you, as you decipher what your partner's aura is revealing about their overall health and well-being.

You may also try this exercise to see and read your own aura. To do this, find an area where there is a large mirror that is placed in opposition to a white or light, neutral-colored wall. Stand against the wall, in front of the mirror, and gaze at your reflection. Using the eye fixation technique, focus on the outer silhouette of your body. You will begin to see the colors of your own aura shifting and changing. Notice if there are any dark, murky areas where the energy seems to be blocked. You will want to make a note of any perceived areas of dysfunction. Take time to draw your impressions on a tablet using colored pencils. This will give you a chance to further examine what your aura is revealing about you.

The strength of your aura is an indicator of your overall physical, emotional, and spiritual well-being. You will want to do all that you can to maintain the strongest aura possible. The aura can be weakened by many things, such as stress, poor diet, and lack of sleep. Negative emotions, such as anger, worry, and fear also weaken the aura. Consuming drugs and alcohol can create holes in the aura, leaving a person vulnerable to unwanted outside energies. Ways that you can strengthen your aura include choosing to be around happy people, thinking positive thoughts, exercising regularly, eating nourishing food, drinking lots of water, meditating daily, singing, wearing protective crystals, and taking salt baths. All of these things will help to strengthen your aura and leave you feeling renewed and revitalized.

Before anything manifests in the physical body, it manifests first in the aura. A medical clairvoyant can see dark, dense smudges or grey clouds over areas of the body that are in need of healing. There may be an area of muddied static energy over a particular chakra, indicating the presence of disease in a corresponding organ. For example, if a person has a predisposition to weak kidneys, you might observe an area of dull-colored energy over their second chakra. If someone is experiencing anger or rage, this may show up in as a jagged, dark-reddish bolt of energy over the first chakra. The human aura reflects one's physical and emotional well being. It is also an indicator of where one may have become stuck. The energetic field of shifting light that surrounds the body reflects a person's passion, joy, pain, and sorrow.

You can practice looking at auras anywhere, at any time. When you find yourself standing in line, while at the grocery store, bank, or post office; this offers you an opportunity to practice reading auras. You can also observe auras when you spend time in nature. Take time to notice the auras of the flowers, the trees, the mountains, the birds, and the animals. Your perception of the world will expand as you become more and more attuned to the energy fields that surround all of creation.

*"The best way to predict the future is to create it."*
*-Abraham Lincoln*

# Chapter 22
## Creating Your Future

The future is in your hands and it is up to you to create the life you desire. Whether you realize it or not, you are currently creating your future in this present moment. Every thought you think, every decision you make, every goal you set, every fear you allow into your consciousness, every action you take, is determining what your tomorrow will look like.

Have you ever struggled with making a major decision about something that could potentially alter the course of your life? When you are faced with a life-changing decision such as whether or not you should move to a new place, take a new job, get married, or embark upon a journey, these decisions can be paralyzing.

I know, for myself, that I have often oscillated back and forth, in an effort to make the right decision about something. I have driven myself crazy and felt completely overwhelmed as I've gone through the arduous process of weighing one option against another, all the while fearing that I might be making the wrong choice. Over the years, I have discovered a technique that assists me in the decision-making process. This technique has enabled me to guide my future with confidence. It helps me to anticipate, how the choices I make, will result in certain outcomes that may or may not be right for me.

The secret to foreseeing a future outcome, before embarking on a new endeavor, is to walk through the prospective scenario in your imagination beforehand. When you do this, it is important to immerse yourself and sense every detail about the experience, with great clarity. Having a vision for your life should be the foundation and reference point for every decision you make.

You may want to create a vision board to help you envision your life in all areas; including family, career, relationships, finances, and lifestyle. Begin with a blank slate using a large poster-board, and then, fill it with images that represent what you desire to see in your future. You can either cut out images from magazines or draw and paint your own. When you have a clear vision of what you want in life, this will create a paradigm for the Universe to fill.

Sometimes, even though you might have a vision of what you want your future to look like; it can seem overwhelming to try and figure out where to begin and how to move forward to achieve your dreams. Rather than looking at the colossal picture that can seem so intimidating, it helps to break things down into small increments and set goals that are easy to achieve. Start where you are, and be brave enough to take the first step. Focus on one step at a time and before you know it, you will arrive at your destination.

Before you embark on making a dream come true, be certain that your dream is worthy of your endeavors and commitment. If you are feeling hesitation, examine any self-doubts or limiting beliefs that are standing in your way. It is imperative that you acknowledge and remove all of the self-imposed barriers that are lingering in your mind. Listen with your heart to your inner voice. If the path is right for you, doors will open easily and you will be guided. Rise above limitations and trust that the Universe is supporting you, clearing a path towards your destiny.

## Meditation to Create Your Own Future

Begin by getting meditative. Close your eyes and quiet your mind. Take some slow, deep breaths. When you feel completely relaxed, direct your attention to your third eye. Project an image onto the screen of your mind that is indicative of your current situation. In your mind's eye, use your imagination to transport yourself to the future that you would like to explore. As you arrive in this potential future, make an effort to perceive how the environment feels to you. Do you feel safe? Notice the texture of the air, and breathe in the smells and fragrances. Feel the earth under your feet. The more specific you are, the more accurate you will be in assessing your feelings and observations.

Next, check in with your heart space and feel the energies of the people that you encounter. How are you being received by others in this potential scenario? Are you feeling loved and supported, or are you feeling ignored and disconnected? Does the environment feel friendly or does it feel hostile? Imagine walking the streets and entering your future home. How does it feel? Examine every feeling that you experience.

At last, imagine that you are at the end of your life. Look back over your life and ask yourself if you have any regrets about any decisions you have made. Do you have regrets about where you chose to live, or the person you chose to marry, or whether or not you chose to have children? Do you have regrets about how you spent your time; either working too much, not traveling enough, or not spending enough time with certain people? Take note of any regrets that you want to avoid. When you are finished with your visualization, return to the present moment.

This meditation will help you get a sense of whether a particular decision will move you forward in the direction of dreams. You will gain clarity on whether a decision is really right for you or not. The use of this technique will spare you from unnecessary struggles and diversions as you consciously create your future.

*"It's never too late to be what you might have been."*
*-George Eliot*

# Chapter 23
## Healing Your Past

The past is a personal set of memories that shapes our beliefs about who we are. Even though the past no longer exists; unsettled memories can still intrude into our lives and cause anguish, inhibiting us from fulfilling our dreams. To avoid this pitfall, we need to be aware of the hang-ups we still carry with us and the hindrances that occupy our minds. We need to examine the past and understand how it is still affecting us today.

People tend to get stuck in behaviors that no longer serve them. They respond to life's current situations, using old, worn-out coping mechanisms. These habitual thought-patterns and knee-jerk reactions play out over-and-over again and always lead to the same outcomes. When someone becomes trapped in a repetitive, destructive mindset and continues to respond to situations in an unhealthy reactive manner; it makes it very difficult to change the paradigm and imagine a brighter future.

Throughout my own life, I have struggled with these issues. In an attempt to discover how to become free of the painful memories that have inhibited me from expressing my soul's light, I set out on a search to discover how I can truly heal from my broken past and become whole. It has been a lifelong journey of self-discovery; an expedition that has led me to delve deep into my soul, to uncover the essence of who I am and recover the joyful innocence of the child who was left behind.

When you make the decision to unearth and transform your own past, you begin a journey of self-empowerment and profound healing. As you face your pain, you will be able to recognize and break through the barriers in your mind that have been holding you back. You will find freedom from the emotional and psychological blockages that have kept you imprisoned and inhibited you from living a full and inspired life.

You have the power to transform your own past. It all comes down to changing your perception about what has gone before. When you are able to change the story in your mind, your narrative will also change. You can rise above the circumstances you were born into, and know that the past does not define you. When you are able to forgive everyone for everything, you set your spirit free. Let go of the memories that steal your joy.

## Meditation to Forgive and Release the Past

The following meditation will guide you to release your past and retrieve your power. To begin this process, close your eyes and take ten slow, deep breaths; exhaling fully after each breath. When you recognize that you are at a deeper level of mind, prepare yourself to take a journey through time. Allow yourself to drift back to the period before you were born. Envision yourself as a soul of pure light, hovering in space; preparing to inhabit the body that is being prepared for you, in your future mother's womb. You can imagine that as a freshly cleansed soul, ready to begin a new life; you would be slipping in and out of the developing body that would soon be yours for a lifetime. Your soul would be connecting to the energy of those individuals, already in human form, who are destined to share your life with you; such as your future parents and family members.

From an elevated viewpoint, contemplate the purpose of your upcoming incarnation. What obstacles will you be facing that will challenge your soul, to help you grow in wisdom? Orient your consciousness toward the physical plane and try to get a sense of whether you will be welcomed or rejected. How do your parents feel about your impending birth? Become aware of how your consciousness is absorbing your mother's energy frequency. Take note of how her thoughts and feelings are affecting you. Are you receiving life-affirming vibrations?

As you continue your meditation, project an image of your mother upon the screen of your mind. Visualize her as a young woman, waiting to give birth to you. Contemplate what her life was like at that point in time. Was she happy to be carrying you in her womb? Was she scared? Did she have the support of family and friends? Were you a wanted child? What was her financial situation? What was your mother's relationship with your father like? Did they love each other? Was your mother nourishing herself with good food or was she engaging in detrimental behavior during her pregnancy? All of these factors played a significant role and yielded great influence over your physiological and emotional well-being; as you absorbed your mother's energy and feelings as your own. The emotional environment, that surrounded your birth, colored your perception about your own self-worth, before you were even born.

As you do this exercise; when you bring up the image of your mother in your mind's eye, make it a point to include every detail you can remember. As you look upon her with love and compassion; with each incoming breath, breathe in love and with each exhale, breathe out healing. Do this a number of times until you feel a sense of peace.

Next, in your mind's eye, allow the image of your mother to change into an image of her as a small child. See her as an innocent little girl, and try to understand what life was like for her. Send love to that little child from your heart. As you develop empathy for your mother, it will become easier for you to let go of any resentments and regrets that you may have been holding onto, and come to a place of peace and complete forgiveness. This exercise will help you to uncover and heal your deepest core wounds.

Repeat this meditation process to heal issues with your father. How did he feel about your impending birth? Was he apprehensive, worried about how he was going to be able to support you? Was he willing to take on the emotional task to be a supportive force in your life? Was he mature and responsible or was he acting juvenile in his ways? As you observe him in your mind's eye, breathe in love with each incoming breath and breathe out healing with each exhale. Visualize your father as a little boy and find compassion in your heart for him as an innocent child. In your mind's eye, forgive and embrace that child. Let go of everything; all resentments and regrets. Once you are able to come to a place in your heart of full forgiveness, you will be free to rise above the mire of perceived shortcomings and resentments that you have been holding onto. You will be able to move forward; with new understanding and appreciation, and recognize your parents as pure beings of light on a sacred soul journey. You can apply this meditation to heal any relationship and resolve the pain you still carry from the past.

As you heal your heart and make it a practice to observe the inner light in every individual, you will begin to instigate changes in the energy around you. When you honor and encourage the light in another person, you help them to shine brighter and the world becomes a better place.

Engage in this process of observation and forgiveness; starting from the time you were a child and move forward through all of the years of your life that have led up to this day. As you revisit events from the past, make it a practice to forgive and let go. With this meditation, you are unwinding the chains that have inhibited you from expressing your soul's true light.

*"If you want love and abundance in your life, give it away."*
*-Mark Twain*

# Chapter 24

## Infinite Abundance

Wealth is a state of mind. Every aspect of your life is defined by your mindset. Your beliefs regarding money and abundance are a determining factor in achieving personal financial success and enjoying a life of plenty. As you create your reality by the thoughts that you think and the expectations you have, the Universe will match your expectations. If you believe that money is scarce and hard to come by, and that there will never be enough to fill your needs; your belief will be reflected in the reality that appears before you. On the other hand, if you set out to pursue your dreams, and trust that the financial resources you require will be available when needed; the Universe will respond in kind.

The truth is that we all need money to live on. There is no reason to feel apologetic for achieving financial success, living a life of comfort, and having your needs met. Money is energy. It is neither good nor bad. For some of us, however, it brings up feelings of fear, guilt, and anxiety. These negative emotions are self-defeating and are the result of an internal mindset that was formed at some point in the past. This faulty mindset needs to be scrutinized and unraveled in order to understand where the apprehension, regarding wealth and abundance, is coming from.

Above all, in order to have prosperity in your life, you must believe that you are worthy. You can change your paradigm by becoming aware of your fears and the ways in which you might be sabotaging your own success. You can begin to dismantle your defeating beliefs by bringing them to the light; and replacing worn-out inhibiting patterns, with new ways of thinking. This is the beginning of creating a new mindset that will change your life from the inside out.

Take a moment to reflect on your own beliefs about money and abundance. Where did these beliefs originate? Most likely you adopted some of these beliefs from your parents. What were their attitudes toward money? Was there a fear of lack? Was there tension in the household due to worries about money?

When people get stuck in the mindset of "poverty consciousness" and are afraid that they will never have enough to meet their needs; the flow of wealth is hindered, as the Universe responds and matches their expectations. The reason for this is that their fears of living in poverty are dictating their story. Adopting the right mindset, that attracts abundance, is a tricky thing. The inclination to go to great lengths to be thrifty, in order to save money, seems logical; but in actuality, pinching every penny stops the flow of energy and reinforces the illusion of scarcity. In truth, the abundance of the Universe is infinite. It is only the "fear of lack" that creates the false impression that it is necessary to struggle for everything one gets in life. This fear sets off a kind of frenzy to hoard resources in order to provide for oneself and their family. This is how greed is born. Greed is a mindset that reflects the fear of poverty.

The quest for money is a driving force that motivates behavior. As an observer; I have seen the underlying games that people play, to align themselves with the right people and situations that they perceive will make them wealthy. Oftentimes, this tactic involves suppressing and crushing others in an effort to rise to the top. When it comes to acquiring wealth; some people are willing to do whatever they believe it takes to succeed, no matter how vicious and heartless they have to be.

This is simply not necessary. There is another way to approach things. As I've mentioned before, the laws of the spiritual world, work differently than one would expect. In the case of acquiring wealth and abundance, it isn't a matter of holding on, but rather a matter of letting go. The following story is an example of how the energy of money works.

Several years ago, my husband and I set out to create our own business, a software development company. When we first started the company, money was tight. Each month, when it was time to pay the bills, we barely managed to meet the minimum payments. We lived as frugally as possible, yet there was always a certain amount of stress and tension, as we worried about how to make ends meet.

One day, I decided to take a leap of faith and try a different approach, in the way I was dealing with our finances. Instead of carefully accounting for every dime, I decided to let go of my fear of poverty and replace my mindset with the belief that the abundance of the Universe is infinite. I began to donate money to charitable causes. Whenever I received a donation request for a cause that I believed in, I would write a check for a small amount. I decided not to worry about how things were going to work out, but instead, I extended my heart and my wallet to those in need. As soon as I did this, everything began to change.

Money began to come in from unexpected sources. Out of the blue, people began to promote our software. Our company was featured as one of the top software providers in the industry. All of a sudden, orders were pouring in as fast as we could fill them. As a result, money began to flow into our lives effortlessly. Before long, all of the bills were paid and we were able to buy our dream home. All of this happened, as soon as I made the simple decision to stop holding on so tightly to money and I allowed the energy of abundance to flow. It really does work!

Generosity is moving from separateness to embracing all of humanity as a family. One generous gesture can change a person's life. When you make a decision to serve a higher purpose to help uplift others, you will attract abundance into your life. What goes around comes around. The laws of karma are exact. When you give your time, love, energy, or financial support to help others, you initiate a wave of prosperity that will eventually come back to you. As you do this, you will notice an energy shift, as the tide of abundance returns to fill your life effortlessly. When you change your thoughts, the vibrations around you will also change. The law of abundance states that when you work for the good of all people, and you send out mental images of love and abundance; whatever you send out will come back to you ten thousand fold.

The Universe is infinitely abundant. There is no reason to believe in scarcity. Whenever you find yourself in need of something; relax, have faith, and visualize with clarity exactly what you want. When you do this, be very precise about everything you wish for and the Universe will respond in kind. As you endeavor to create your new reality, the more details you can envision the better. Believe that you are worthy to receive abundance in your life. See it clearly and then step out of the way. You must let go to open the flow. Expect miracles!

*"Carry your heart through this world like  
a life-giving sun."*  
*- Hafiz*

# Chapter 25
## Lead With Your Heart

The heart is a gateway to Universal Love. It is a holy place where the physical body merges with the Divine. Within the heart, there is a sacred space of infinite love and compassion. The heart receives and amplifies love from the Universe; and sends it out into the world by means of electromagnetic energy waves.

Your heart holds the beautiful essence of the light and the love that you are. In order to share your radiance with the world, it is important to know and understand the true power of your own heart. In addition to being a miraculous muscle that beats to sustain life, the heart is also known as the seat of the soul. Since ancient times, many cultures and traditions, including the Egyptians, the Hindus, and the Aztecs, have all held the belief that the soul resides within the heart. It is regarded as the primary interface between the non-physical and physical worlds.

There are three different components that make up the heart. There is a physical component, an emotional component, and a spiritual component. As we all know, the physical heart is an amazing muscle that keeps us alive. It is the first organ to form in the developing fetus. Beginning at approximately six weeks after conception, the heart begins to beat in the embryo. Soon after, the blood and circulatory system starts to form, powered by the heart. The blood carries nutrients to keep the cells alive, enabling the fetus to grow and survive. The heart continues its important job of pumping blood, throughout a lifetime.

In addition to being a remarkable muscle that ensures our survival, the heart is a sensory organ that receives and processes information. Researchers have discovered that the heart actually has its own brain that connects to the nervous system. The "heart-brain" is composed of neurons, neurotransmitters, proteins, and support cells, like those found in the brain. This enables the heart to learn, remember, and make functional decisions. The heart is endowed with consciousness. It takes in information from the surrounding environment and sends signals to the brain that trigger biochemical, neurological, biophysical, and energetic responses; which in turn serve to regulate the body. The heart and the brain are in constant communication with each other.

Using modern scientific instruments to measure magnetic energy fields, researchers have discovered that the heart is the most powerful generator of electromagnetic energy in the human body. The energy field of the heart is about sixty times stronger than the energy field produced by the brain. Electromagnetic energy is generated by means of nerve impulses; creating waves of energy that pass from one end of a nerve cell to another. These electromagnetic waves reach far beyond the body. Not only do these waves travel through the air and through solid materials; but they also travel through the vacuum of space. This means that the heart's energy can reach across great distances.

As you become conscious of the energetic emissions of your own heart; you can direct this energy consciously to help uplift others and facilitate healing. When you offer your attention to another person, this is an act of love. When you share the energy from your heart, along with loving, healing thoughts that go out from your mind; you exert a profound, positive impact on the energy fields of everyone around you. In accessing the powers of your heart and mind, you have the resources to illuminate the Universe.

The heart is also the source of emotions. It is the point of awareness where feelings enter the body. Feelings are the language of the soul. It is from the sacred space of the heart that we "feel life".

Our hearts skip a beat when we fall in love. We hold others in our hearts, and we become heartbroken when things fall apart.

When an issue comes up for you and you are trying to make a decision about something, pay attention to your feelings. In every moment, you have a choice on how you choose to respond to any situation. You may choose to react by opening your heart in love or closing your heart in fear. The energy that you exude in your response to life, has a tremendous impact on your own physical health and emotional well being. When you make life-affirming choices, stemming from the force of love, you build and strengthen your physical and emotional bodies; whereas if you respond to life with fearful reactions such as jealousy, hate, and resentment, and insist on holding onto grudges, you weaken your physical and emotional bodies. Every choice you make creates the energy of the next moment.

In addition to the physical and emotional aspects of the heart, there is a spiritual component. The heart is the seat of the soul. Within your heart is the bridge to the Universe, where you are given unlimited access to the infinite field of love. Your heart and soul operate together. When you listen to your heart, you will hear the spirit of guidance. Learn to trust your heart's wisdom and allow your heart to guide you. The voice of your heart is the voice of your soul. When you listen to this voice, you will receive a great sense of clarity. You can trust that your soul will always guide you towards your highest path, on your way to fulfill your destiny.

## Heart Meditation

Take a moment to meditate on your own heart space. When you tune into your heart, you are tuning into your higher-self. You are connecting to your soul, the non-physical part of you that is eternal. Close your eyes and place your hands on your heart. Feel the strength and the power of your heartbeat. Ask your heart to speak to you. In doing so, forgotten memories and suppressed emotions will begin to stir and rise to the surface. As your heart reveals your deepest truth, you will gain insight into the buried feelings, memories, and regrets that are dimming the expression of your soul's light. When an unprocessed emotion or memory comes up, be willing to sit with it. Acknowledge your feelings and how the memory is affecting you. As you breathe in gently, imagine that you are breathing in the light of love. Hold your breath for a few seconds and allow love to fill your being. As you exhale, let go of every emotion that you have been holding onto. Imagine your pain as a healing mist exiting your body. Continue to breathe in love, and breathe out healing; until you feel like you have come to a place of complete serenity and forgiveness. As you are able to release the tension around an event, you will begin to feel your heart's rhythm change and there will be more harmony within your whole being. Each time you do this exercise, you open your heart to the flow of love a little bit more and you invite peace into your life.

As you step out to greet humanity with each new day, make the choice to lead with your heart. When you give your love freely, you will attract more love into your life. Love the world passionately, as if it's the last chance you will ever have. People around you will feel and respond to your positive, magnetic vibration as your loving energy helps to create a more joyful world.

Let love be your guide. Whenever you are unsure of how to react in any given situation, ask yourself, "What would Love do?" Love is patient and kind. Be kind to others as well as yourself. Let love pervade your conversations and filter through your heart before you act or speak. Try to be understanding even when you are in disagreement with others. Hold the awareness in your heart that we are all kindred souls on the path to enlightenment.

When you open your heart to others and suddenly realize that there are no others, but rather that we are all One; then you have taken a huge leap in consciousness. In truth, there is no separation.

As you embrace the entire world with a loving, grateful heart, you invite miracles into your life. Lead with your heart and know that you are held in the arms of Spirit and you will always have the love of the Universe supporting you.

*"Stop acting so small. You are the universe in ecstatic motion.*
*- Rumi*

# Chapter 26
## Raise Your Vibration

Personal vibration refers to the rate at which the electrons spin around the nucleus, in the atoms that make up one's being. One significant factor, that determines how fast or slow the electrons are spinning, is the density of one's consciousness. Essentially, the more a person is in touch is with their higher self, the higher their vibration will be. High vibrations are associated with positive qualities such as love, peace, compassion, and forgiveness. People who carry a high vibration tend to be nurturing, empathetic, enthusiastic about life, highly creative, energetic, physically fit, and emotionally balanced.

On the contrary, people who emanate a low vibration, oftentimes appear to be fatigued, lethargic, and depressed. They may feel stuck in life, with an inability to feel inspired, or open to new possibilities. Bottled up emotions such as guilt, resentment, jealousy, and hate, accumulate like smog between the wide-open spaces of the electrons, thus slowing them down. This, in turn, has an effect on the physical body. A person with low vibration may experience physical symptoms such as headaches, digestive issues, skin problems, or frequent illnesses. When an individual is able to release the pain of their past, the atoms that make up the body are able to contain more light and the density is lifted. This results in the restoration of physical strength and emotional balance as the chakras are able to carry more light.

If you aspire to be an effective channel for bringing God's love and healing light into the world, it is important to adopt daily practices that will assist you in raising your vibration consciously.

When you do this, the God force within you will be intensified. As you fill yourself with light, your presence alone will create a rippling effect; spreading your vibrations of love in waves across the Universe. These energetic waves will touch and influence all those around you on a subtle level. You will discover that your energy has a profound effect on the well-being of others. You have the power to create change and instigate miracles. Stay centered in Spirit. Offer yourself as a channel for love to find its way into this world.

Whenever you have an interaction with another person, you are essentially interacting with their aura or energy field. This energy exchange happens on a subconscious level. When two auras blend or merge, it causes a transfer of energy from one person to another. This is how healing works. A healer with strong energy can transfer healing to someone who is weaker. When you give somebody a hug, you are transmitting healing love and light. If you give someone a smile, most likely that person will pass it on to others.

Not only does your energy have an impact on other people, but the vibration that you carry in any one moment will be mirrored back to you. Whenever things in your life seem chaotic or out of balance, it's a signal for you to check in with your own energy field and become aware of how your own vibration might be contributing to the energy that is manifesting around you. There are a number of things you can do to raise your vibration and restore harmony in your life.

## Seek Solace in Nature

One simple way to increase your vibration is to go out and spend time in nature. When you commune with the natural world, it helps you to connect with the essence of your soul. Whenever you align with the earth, the sky, the rivers, and trees; you tap into the heartbeat of the planet and your consciousness is elevated. Your priorities shift as your perception of the world changes. The mundane thoughts, that so often preoccupy your mind, slip away. You realize that the only thing that truly matters is what is happening in the present moment; for the current moment is the only reality that exists.

In nature, you will find the purest expression of God. The wind that blows like a rushing wave through the trees is the breath of divinity. When you attune yourself to nature, your vibration increases as the Spirit of Life flows into you and pulses through your veins unencumbered. In taking time to be still, while observing all of the subtleties of the natural world around you; the energy of life will fill you and the love in your heart will expand and radiate like a sun from within your being.

## A Meditation to Raise Your Vibration

This meditation will help you to deepen your connection with the natural world and raise your vibration. Begin by finding a serene, peaceful place. If possible, try to find a place where you can sit by a river. If there are no rivers or creeks nearby, you will have to conjure up a river in your imagination. Sit down and become still and meditative. Close your eyes and begin to breathe slowly in and out. Gaze gently through your third eye and observe the images that appear on the inner screen of your mind. The Universe will speak to you in pictures. Notice the symbols that come into your inner sight. These pictograms bring messages pertinent to your life's current situation. You may discover an answer to a problem that has been plaguing you, or gain new insight into a situation that will ultimately lead you to a higher understanding of your life's purpose.

Next, visualize a river of pure white light entering through your crown chakra at the top of your head. This is the healing, cleansing light of God. Allow the light to fill your being. As you sit by the river, place your attention on the sound of the rushing water, and relax as it washes over your senses. Empty your mind and let the river speak to you. You may hear the sound of voices or messages carried on the water. Listen with your whole being. Look within the deep silence to find the peace and the answers that you seek.

Allow the outer world of motors and noise to drift away, as you shift your focus only to nature. Become aware of the bees and the far-off songs of the calling birds that vibrate through the air. As you absorb the primordial power around you, take a deep breath. Imagine that you are breathing in pure light, and say, "I accept the love and light of God". Hold your breath for a few seconds and contemplate the notion that you are one with all of existence. As you exhale, say, "I extend the love and light of God". Focus on compassion for all living things, as you allow the highest power in the Universe to fill your being and flow out from your heart.

## The Transformative Power of Light and Sound

The energy of creation consists of light and sound. The world, as we know it, is a reflection of infinite combinations of light and sound patterns. Our bodies exist as a conglomeration of light and sound waves. The "Universal Law of Vibration" states that anything that exists in our Universe, whether seen or unseen, when broken down to it's purest and most basic form, consists of pure energy or light that resonates as a vibratory frequency or pattern.

Sound has the ability to affect any form that it comes into contact with, by exposing that form to a different rate of frequency vibration. As sound passes through matter, it has a transformative effect. Experiments have revealed that passing high-frequency sound waves through sand will cause the sand to move into sacred geometrical patterns.

One way that you can use the power of sound to raise your vibratory frequency is by immersing yourself in music. When you listen to beautiful music or play an instrument, you raise your own vibration and the vibratory rate of the environment around you. Singing kirtans, chanting mantras, or playing bells, chimes or singing bowls has the same effect. It helps to gather with people you resonate with, to create uplifting music together

Every living thing responds to the effects of sound. Research has shown that plants respond to beautiful music and grow better. Animals respond to music as well, just as humans do. The nervous system entrains to sound frequencies. Certain types of music have a soothing and relaxing effect that can slow down the heart rate, lower blood pressure and give one a sense of well-being. Other types of music can either have a disruptive or stimulating effect. For this reason, it's important to be aware of the sound vibrations around you. If you want to raise your vibration, immerse yourself in music that fills your soul.

## Practice Daily Meditation

Practicing meditation is an effective way to align with your soul's purpose. The act of meditating slows down the brain waves and induces a mode of consciousness that enables you to transcend the physical world and see things from an elevated view. During meditation, you will be able to see life as an objective observer; rather than as a helpless victim caught up in a storm. Meditation offers inner peace and helps to calm the mind, increasing clarity and purpose. This leads to greater awareness.

When you choose to include meditation in your daily life, profound changes will occur. During meditation, you can engineer your life and set the stage, using the power of your mind with focused intention, to create exactly what it is that you want.

Some people may perceive that meditation is too difficult or they may feel that they are not capable of sitting for long periods of time in order to quiet their minds. These are needless stumbling blocks, as there are many different types of meditation that a person may engage in. In essence, meditation is simply a practice in "being present".

You can practice a kind of moving meditation simply by walking on the earth with awareness. Focus your mind on the present moment and let go of all thoughts of worry and judgment. Pay attention to your breath as you breathe gently, in and out. Take in the sensations of life around you. In order to achieve inner peace, it is important to remain open and approach each moment with mindfulness and a kind, gentle heart. There are many forms of meditation that you may want to explore, in order to discover what kind of meditation practice is most suitable for you.

## The Alchemy of Movement

Our bodies are designed to move. The importance of engaging in some sort of daily exercise cannot be underestimated. Movement strengthens the heart and forces the lungs to work harder, in order to move the breath. This, in turn, energizes the body by oxygenating the blood, bringing vital nourishment to all of the cells. Participating in some form of exercise each day is also essential for mental health, as the mind and the body are intimately connected.

Any kind of movement practice or exercise that you choose to engage in will help you to develop strength and agility. This in turn, will make you feel more energetic, confident, capable, and empowered. Movement aids in triggering the release of particular hormones and cell signals. For example, it raises serotonin levels in the brain. Serotonin is the "feel good" hormone that elevates the mood and increases a sense of well-being. Movement cleanses our bodies of accumulated toxins and assists in helping to release emotional trauma. As I've mentioned in previous chapters, unprocessed emotions can become locked in the tissues of our bodies. Conscious movement helps to free the body, mind, and spirit. Regular exercise supports brain health by assisting new neurons to grow and thrive.

There are many ways to incorporate movement into your life. You can choose a gentle movement practice such as Tai-Chi,

Qi-Gong or Yoga, or you can choose something more invigorating. This is an individual choice. Any movement practice or exercise that you choose to engage in, will benefit your body, mind, and spirit.

## Give Yourself to Love

The greatest power in the Universe is love. Awaken from the illusion of separateness, and offer yourself to the world as a force for God's love. You will be guided to go where you are needed most. Trust that God has a plan for you. Be willing to serve and you will be guided. When you radiate your light outward from your heart, you become a walking star; a way shower who can illuminate the path for others. Always remember that your light is who you are!

# A Note to the Reader

This book began with a blank page and a stirring in my soul. A persistent, inner nudging from an unseen force, beckoned me unrelentingly, to share my truth and my journey. Finally, heeding the call, I began to put pen to paper; unsure of the final outcome and where it all would lead. I soon discovered, that each time I sat down to write, it became a kind of therapy for me; as I engaged in back and forth conversations with my higher-self. I dove headfirst into uncovering and sharing my deepest truths while the Universe supported me, consistently urging me onward. As one chapter after another emerged from the depths of my consciousness; lessons and situations in my daily life would appear, coincide, and play out; illustrating to me exactly what I needed to learn most. In the end, this book has become a friend; a trusted confidant to remind me of what is real and what is truly important. I offer this book as a gift. It is the voice of my soul. May it help to light your way.

Made in United States
North Haven, CT
21 November 2022